BREAKING STRONGHOLDS

Sue B. Gelzon

Breaking Strongholds

How Spiritual Warfare Sets Captives Free

Tom White

VINE
BOOKS

Servant Publications
Ann Arbor, Michigan

Vine Books is an imprint of Servant Publications especially
designed to serve evangelical Christians.

Unless otherwise noted, all Scripture quotations in this book
are from the *Holy Bible, New International Version.* Copyright ©
1973, 1978, 1983 Internation Bible Society. Used by permission
of Zondervan Bible Publishers.

Published by Servant Publications
P.O. Box 8617
Ann Arbor, Michigan 48107

Cover design by Michael Andaloro

       96 97 10 9 8 7 6 5

Printed in the United States of America
ISBN 0-89283-782-9

Library of Congress Cataloging-in-Publication Data

White, Tom. 1947–
   Breaking strongholds : how spiritual warfare sets captives free /
Tom White.
   223 p. cm.
   ISBN 0-89283-782-9
   1. Spiritual warfare. 2. Evangelistic work. I. Title.
BV4509.5.W455   1993
235'.4—dc20   92–46735

Dedication

This project has emerged from the crucible of learning how to help fellow pilgrims find the path that leads through the darkness to the light of heaven's door. Such an endeavor is wrought with a mysterious mix of blessing and burden. Blessings are richer when shared, burdens easier when carried with a friend.

"Two can accomplish more than twice as much as one,
for the results can be much better.
If one falls, the other pulls him up;
but if a man falls when he is alone, he's in trouble...
One standing alone can be attacked and defeated,
but two can stand back-to back and conquer;
three is even better, but a triple braided cord
is not easily broken." **Ecclesiastes 4:9, 10, 12 (TLB)**

For the purity of her devotion to Christ, her ceaseless companionship, and her prevailing intercession, I dedicate this work and its fruit to Terri, my incurably cheerful wife and life confidant.
And I thank God for the helping presence of his Spirit who, with Terri, has given us the strength of a triple-braided cord.

Contents

INTRODUCTION

Breaking Strongholds: How Spiritual Warfare Can Set Captives Free

JESUS OF NAZARETH OFTEN ASKED provocative questions. After a number of dramatic episodes in his ministry, the Lord asked his disciples, "Who do people say the Son of Man is?" They posed several safe, credible possibilities. Then Peter blurted out the truth: "You are the Christ, the Son of the Living God."

The Master made it clear that Peter's confession did not originate with human cleverness but was a gift from heaven. Then Jesus spoke a profound revelation: "And I tell you that you are Peter, and *on this rock I will build my church, and the gates of Hades will not overcome it.* I will give you the keys of the kingdom of heaven; whatever you bind on earth will be bound in heaven, and whatever you loose on earth will be loosed in heaven" (Mt 16:18, 19, emphasis mine).

What did Jesus mean by the word "rock"? I am convinced that it is Peter's divinely inspired confession that Jesus is the Messiah, against whom the powers of hell have no hope of prevailing. This "rock" is the unshakeable, historical reality that Jesus alone is the Christ, fully God, fully man, and the source of eternal redemption. The "keys of the kingdom" reside in the spiritual authority delegated to the disciple for representing the Master's kingdom on earth. The follower of Christ bears the awesome privilege of restraining evil and releasing the redemptive presence of the Holy Spirit to build the church.

"I will build my church...." Here we are, closing out the 1990s and closing in on the commencement of the third millennium of church history. As evangelically committed Christians, we find ourselves in stiff competition with secularism, a scientific worldview, and a potpourri of alternative supernatural groups and gurus saying, "This is the way." And every day, people plod by you and me trying their best to make sense of it all. These are the days of deception Jesus and his Apostles warned us about. But today is also the day of salvation for those whom the Lord is calling to himself.

This book is for the serious and seeking Christian who is alive in the Lord and who is aware that this life is a battleground for determining people's destiny in the life to come. I appeal to the believers who say, "Something significant is going on in our world today—God is on the move, and I want to be a part of it." If you're weary of doing ministry in your own power and want to walk in the anointing of the Spirit of God and see some fresh fruit, I challenge you to dig in and learn how to pray in greater authority to set others free from the snares of the adversary.

Have you ever found yourself in a public situation minding your own business when the Lord suddenly surprised you with a divine appointment? Here's one of mine I'll not soon forget. Midway from Denver to Minneapolis on an earlybird flight, I finally woke up enough to put some final touches on a teaching outline for a prayer conference at which I was to speak. The flight was full. I squinched up alongside the window and looked dutifully occupied. Then it happened. The woman next to me pulled out her New Age book. Suddenly I was on assignment. "What are you reading? It looks interesting." (The hook.) "Oh, it's a self-help thing—how to realize the potential of your inner self." (The opening.) She and her husband were en route to a conference sponsored by a major metaphysical group based in Minneapolis.

The conversation was rapid and intense. She quickly caught my drift, but seemed encouraged that I was not a standard "evangelical type." I began relating intelligently to the content of her book. It came as no surprise that she had been seriously soured by Christians. Her words were all too familiar: "We had a bad experience with the church years ago. We decided to take a new direction." She had been disillusioned, driven away by a caricature of the Lord Jesus. The Holy Spirit then orchestrated every word, every nuance of our chat. Though appearing disinterested, with no eye contact, her husband was clearly taking it all in.

We went point for point, distinguishing the biblical Jesus from New Age "Christ," sin and separation from a personal God from an indwelling "god" waiting to be discovered, the authority of the Bible from endless truth-telling books written by the latest gurus or dictated by disembodied spiritual masters. I worked gently at representing my Jesus as opposed to her caricature of him. I discovered that this woman's daughter was an evangelical Christian preparing for the ministry. (The personal pain opening.) "How do you and your daughter get along? Don't you have a lot of tension over these things?"

We began our descent into Minneapolis. I told her I would pray that God would guide her into truth and challenged her to read the Bible with a fresh and open mind. Then I prayed silently, asking God to subdue the influence of deception and to lead her into the light of the truth. When we landed, I said good-bye.

Many of us want to step outside of our comfort zones and be used by God to touch others for eternity. To do so, we need to move from simply understanding the principles of truth to walking in its power. The Holy Spirit, the Spirit of truth, is speaking to the church today. He is calling God's people to prayer and praise and equipping them for spiritual warfare and the coming harvest. Let's talk about his work in terms of "three streams."

Picture three streams converging into one river, steadily widening and deepening. Picture now a deep stream that is rapidly gaining both strength and depth, an outpouring of the Spirit that is unparalleled in church history. Biblically, this may be a fulfillment of the prophecy spoken through Joel (2:28, 29) and re-articulated by Peter (Acts 2:17, 18). God alone knows the meaning and the timing of this fulfillment. *Let's call this stream "experiencing the presence of God through prayer and praise."* Believers in every corner of the kingdom are re-discovering the personal and corporate practice of prayer as a delight rather than a duty. The pure joy of praise and worship permeates countless gatherings. Praise God for this sovereign visitation! Has the Lord Jesus been knocking at your heart's door, nudging you toward deeper intimacy with him? In chapters three, eight, and nine, I'll challenge you to wade deeper into this stream of truth and to believe God for new empowerment.

The second stream, building from a trickle in the early 1980s and still running strong, involves the emphasis on discerning and dealing effectively with the schemes of the counter-kingdom. *Let's call this dimension of truth "understanding and practicing spiritual warfare."* In chapter two, I want to help you understand and overcome hindrances and struggles that relate to personal strongholds in the life of the Christian. Chapters four and five deal with the how-to's of helping non-Christians break free of Satan's deceptions. In chapter six we'll dig into uncovering strongholds within the church. And chapter seven will challenge you to consider involvement in strategic spiritual warfare intercession for communities, nations, and unreached people groups.

The third stream, inclusive of the others, is the focus on getting the gospel to the remaining twelve thousand or so unreached people groups in our world. Most of these peoples live in the "10-40 Window" (North latitudes ten to forty degrees, stretching from North Africa across the Middle East through Asia to the Philippines). Within this window lie some of the more longstanding and formidable satanic strongholds. How will we penetrate them?

Because of our shrinking world, more and more of these people end up on our doorstep. Those who need to hear the Good News are no longer "out there" but in our own neighborhoods and communities. *Let's call this stream "harvest."* I believe the Lord is now prompting those on the cutting edge of missions to pioneer his plan to reach the world before he comes again. In chapters one and ten I'll explain more clearly what this harvest is and how to get more involved.

These three streams, each having its own tributaries, are merging together in marvelous ways. My goal in this book is to promote effective prayer that overcomes the warfare we face in our efforts to loose the unsaved from the grip of the "father of lies" (Jn 8:44).

After Jesus had given authority to overcome all the power of the enemy, the seventy-two disciples returned to report dramatic results: "Lord, even the demons submit to us in your name." Jesus immediately cautioned them, "do not rejoice that the spirits submit to you, but rejoice that your names are written in heaven" (Lk 10:20).

Jesus' response underlines an important point. What is the real purpose of "spiritual warfare"? It is not to display power nor merely to insure personal protection from evil. Spiritual warfare means being compassionately involved in wrenching people free from the prospect of eternal death. We can experience supreme joy knowing that new names are being added to the Lamb's book of life. Life presents us with a variety of personal fulfillments, but for the Christian, the citizen of a higher kingdom, no joy is greater than personally helping a lost pilgrim find his or her way home.

The Lord of the church is looking for everyday people compelled to labor for the liberation of others held captive to the lies of the prince of darkness. The Master Evangelist challenged a fisherman, a tax collector, and other ordinary men and women to "ask the Lord of the harvest to send out workers into his harvest field" (Mt 9:38). Might you be an answer to those prayers?

Today we have before us a window of opportunity, a season

for learning and training. God is raising an army to help set captives free. These are days of prayer and preparation. I believe we will soon see an increased parallel outpouring of power, both satanic and divine. Our God will manifest his glory in the midst of man's mess. What a day to be on the winning side!

In the midst of a wave of numerous books on spiritual warfare, why is it important for you to read this book? Because the wiles of Satan that hinder our efforts to lead people to Jesus have not been adequately dealt with on the practical level. We must understand how to break the power of enemy "strongholds," those lies and half-truths that distort a clear understanding of the gospel.

We need to understand enemy untruths that keep believers sidelined, ineffective in their service. We can do far better at discerning the lies that keep people from embracing truth in Christ. Any Christian firmly grounded in Scripture can detect these kinds of distortions. Any committed believer carries Jesus' authority to combat satanic deception. Why do I make this bold claim? Because the Holy Spirit lives in every believer, giving discernment and authority to lead the lost into the light.

Let me share with you truth that got my attention, that helped me step out in Jesus' authority to tackle and triumph over the strongholds of the evil one. Several nagging questions have at points plagued my first twenty years of Christian service. Why do so many people fail to receive the generous and free gift offered in Jesus Christ? Why do the cults and the occult maintain so strong a grip on seemingly sincere, seeking people? What lies behind the pervasive and persistent bondage that results from family dysfunction, sexual abuse, and compulsive behaviors? How can we hope to penetrate the "tough turf" of resistance in select areas of the mission field?

Are we missing something? I think so. Finding fresh, discerning, and balanced light on spiritual warfare is a key to better answering these questions.

"The gates of hell will not prevail..." More of us need to learn how to move in Jesus' authority. Sensitivity to his Spirit and to human need can open countless doors of opportunity to add people to the community of faith. Are we not called to live a supernatural lifestyle, being responsive to the promptings of the Holy Spirit leading us to cooperate in his mission of releasing people from the bondage to lies and emptiness? Let's take a bold journey together to discover a way of viewing reality that just may revolutionize how you perceive people and will lead you to be a fruit-bearer for the glory of the Father.

1

Setting Prisoners Free: A Missing Dimension

I N THE SPRING OF 1991, I was traveling by train from Vienna to Innsbruck, Austria. Feasting on the spectacular view outside my window, I nibbled the last bits of a granola bar and opened my Bible for devotions. The peace and quiet soon exploded as the train eased into the next station. Bags crashed down from the racks above in the grip of those who were exiting. The lurching rush of new passengers filled the aisle. Head down and eyes fixed, I focused on the words of the psalmist.

As the train jerked and rolled on, something felt quite different in the cabin. I looked up to survey the new passengers, trying not to engage eye contact. Across from me sat a well-dressed woman who gazed resolutely out the window. While she seemed to deny defiantly my very presence, I couldn't help but notice the medallion hanging around her neck.

A strange discomfort settled over me. Having learned to ask the Lord about these kinds of impressions, I prayed silently, "Lord, what is this tension?" I meandered through the Psalms and waited for an answer. Strong words came to me: "metaphysics, spiritism, New Age."

What was going on here? Was I projecting onto this anonymous person my own filter of reality? Was I experiencing a bit of paranoia? Perhaps. Yet I have sought the Lord over many years for a sharpened discernment, the ability to see as he sees, past the typical and touchable things of this earth. No, I wasn't imagining this. A strange spiritual presence had just broken into my personal peace. This woman may have seen the Bible on my lap and registered strong mental resistance, maybe something like "Uh-oh... a Bible-toting evangelical!"

Whatever her thoughts, I felt caught up in what seemed to be a mild power encounter. I began to pray silently as led by the Holy Spirit. *Lord, in Jesus' name, I bring this woman to you as one for whom you died. Please do something in her heart right now. Lead her to someone who knows you, who can speak her language. Holy Spirit, move now to penetrate and expose the darkness around her. Let her sense the power of your presence flowing now through my prayers. Lord, break the power of these spirits. Weaken their grip on her mind and will. Jesus, in your authority, I speak judgment and destruction on the work of the enemy in this woman's life.*

My restful journey through the serene Austrian countryside had unexpectedly shifted to frontline spiritual warfare. This woman remained on the train for only four stops, not once acknowledging my presence across from her. As she prepared to leave, I caught her eye, beamed a quick grin, and sent her out the door with a warm "Auf Wiedersehen!" My readiness as an ambassador for Christ had loosed the Spirit's redemptive presence. I know of no greater fulfillment than being about this kind of kingdom business.

LOOKING AT LIFE THROUGH NEW LENSES

In his parable of the seed and the sower, Jesus mentions a variety of responses to the sowing of the Word of God. The seed that fell alongside the path was eaten by "the birds." Jesus interprets:

"When anyone hears the message about the kingdom and does not understand it, the evil one comes and snatches away what was sown in his heart" (Mt 13:19). Any farmer knows how birds can hinder the productivity of his crops. But we often fail to understand the similar efforts of demonic spirits to hinder the spiritual productivity of the Word of God.

In another parable, Jesus describes the "weeds" among the wheat (Mt 13:24-30). Again, he interprets: "The weeds are the sons of the evil one, and the enemy who sows them is the devil" (13:38b). The devil not only hinders genuine conversions but also promotes counterfeit conversions—the self-righteous and religious who may look like a good crop but lack the life of the Spirit. We need to open our eyes to see the invisible influence of evil spirits as an important element of the resistance in leading people to truth.

Paul confirms this perspective: "the god of this age has blinded the minds of unbelievers, so that they cannot see the light of the gospel of the glory of Christ" (2 Cor 4:4). The language here indicates a blindness resulting from "smoke," an actual clouding of mental discernment, a darkening of intellect. No doubt some of you have encountered such smoke screens when you have come to a point of sharing Christ with someone. Sometimes we detect a hindrance that goes beyond personal opinions.

Describing the preconversion state, Paul tells the Ephesian believers that they once "followed the ways of this world and of the ruler of the kingdom of the air, the spirit who is now at work in those who are disobedient" (Eph 2:2). In some way, to some degree, there is a "spirit" (a subtle power of rebellion) at work in the lives of those separated from the knowledge of Jesus. If the fruits of spiritual harvest are to increase, the church must learn the skills of discernment and authoritative prayer that can pierce these spiritual barriers. Such an approach guided by the Holy Spirit's gifts and graced with his anointing will enable believers to more effectively share the good news.

For the most part, the major focus of Christian ministry has been on evangelism and discipleship. This is well and good. Some inevitably hear the good news, receive it, and grow to be committed disciples. But others can be blinded to the gospel by the deceiver. We need to know when to salt our proclamation with prayer and power rooted in a spiritual authority.

Even if we master the art of sowing gospel seeds, we may lack the spiritual discernment to know when and how to beat back the demonic birds of the air that devour the seed and distract people from embracing Christ as Lord. We can all learn to bind the darkness and loose the light in the lives of those who cross our daily paths.

Matthew offers us a deeper look at the heart of the Master: "When he saw the crowds, he had compassion on them, because they were harassed and helpless, like sheep without a shepherd" (Mt 9:36). Jesus wants to teach us to have the same discerning response to the human condition. As described in the next two verses, the Lord exhorts the disciples to pray for more workers to go into the harvest field and grants the disciples authority over unclean spirits (Mt 9:38-10:1). We too are called to confront whatever evil emissaries keep people bound and blind.

Have the conditions of life changed any since Jesus' ministry? Did only the first disciples receive such authority? No. We are all called to engage in spiritual warfare. Have you ever noticed how much trouble Jesus stirred up whenever he presented truth in the power of the Spirit? He walked in the fullness of truth endowed with divine authority. As his disciple, you can walk in a similar anointing.

Have you ever sat in a public place packed with countless bodies and ringing with noises? How about a college football game or a commuter train station in a metropolitan city? Being surrounded by a swarm of humanity can prompt some serious people-watching in our more pensive moments. The mind of the searching, sensitive Christian may begin to ponder deeper realities: *Lord, how many of these busy people really think seriously about you or the weight of eternal things? How are you going to break into these lives and reveal yourself as the source of life?* Let's bring this closer to home. How about the business colleague, the fellow student, the neighborhood friend, the couple you mingle with in a social setting?

I want to challenge you to look below the surface, to see yourself and others through different lenses. Donning such spiritual spectacles may stretch you a bit but will enable you to perceive more clearly the unseen evil that shapes how ordinary people think and make choices. You will understand more of how evil affects even *you*.

God wants to stir in you a new passion for his presence, an ardent desire to participate in his plan. He wants to use you—*who* you are, *where* you are. In a culture that insists on religious and intellectual tolerance, we are called upon to be truth tellers for God. What an uncomfortable bind! We often draw back from the hard work of digging our plow into rocky soil and scattering the seed. We may be afraid to impose on others. While many Christians feel inadequate and ill-prepared for formal witnessing, we often feel plain awkward about sharing our convictions in a secular climate.

Relax. I'm not going to ask you to become an evangelist. I *am* asking you to open your eyes and your heart, to pray more compassionately and concertedly for those who haven't yet entered into a relationship with Jesus Christ. Our primary call is to bring the presence of Jesus into our everyday interaction with neighbors, colleagues, social contacts, even brief encounters in the shopping mall or at a child's soccer game. We need some fresh light on how to build relational bridges with those who haven't yet met the Savior. We need to learn how to pray for these lost sheep to come to know the Good Shepherd.

God maintains a certain sovereign selectivity in seeking out and pursuing those he wants for himself. Jesus explained to Nicodemus that the working of the Holy Spirit in bringing forth eternal life can be compared with the wind. We cannot know where it comes from or where it goes next. Each person who is touched by the Spirit then bears the sacred responsibility of choosing how to respond.

Jesus' parable of the farmer scattering seed is even more practical. Some seeds produce grain; others wither in the sun or are choked by thorns. Some people are able to believe the message of Christ crucified for sins. Others vehemently reject it. Gimmicks or formulas only muddy the waters of this mysterious flow of salvation. While leaving souls in the hands of God, we can only commit ourselves to do a better job of sowing seed, of living a life worthy of his name, of getting better at beating back the demonic birds that devour the seed. The waging of spiritual warfare remains an especially weak link in our sharing of the gospel.

The Lord is bringing people from every country and culture into relationship with himself. This is the big news, the real news that doesn't make for front page secular headlines. This is the building of the invisible kingdom. As individuals, as small groups, and as corporate fellowships, we must commit ourselves to the kind of prayer that promotes the purposes of heaven. We need to pray in a way that will pierce the hearts of men and women and penetrate the darkness that surrounds them.

Edgardo Silvoso, founder of Harvest Evangelism and a leader of the church growth movement in Argentina, recently shared with me a profoundly simple truth: "We must understand that God is more ready and willing to answer prayer for sheep number one hundred than for our personal needs." This does not mean that God is not invested in taking care of those of us in the fold, but like a good shepherd, he sees that the ninety-nine are safe, and goes out to find that hundredth sheep still threatened by the wolves. How many lost sheep do you know? Look around. Find them. Ask the Shepherd to teach you how to pray them into the fold.

After his temptation in the wilderness, Jesus returned to Galilee to minister "in the power of the Spirit" (Lk 4:14). Entering the synagogue in Nazareth, he stood to recite the daily reading, a text from Isaiah descriptive of the Messiah: "The Spirit of the Lord is on me, because he has anointed me to preach good news to the poor. He has sent me to proclaim freedom for the prisoners and recovery of sight for the blind, to release the oppressed, to proclaim the year of the Lord's favor" (Lk 4:18-19).

The "poor" refers not to economic status but to spiritual poverty. The "good news" involves a restored relationship with God through the forgiveness of sins. We can communicate that message of freedom to people by the way we live and by the words we speak. But even while making an effort to do so, we can fail to appreciate the reality that people are "prisoners" oppressed by a foreign power.

Not until Jesus appears in the power of the Spirit do we see this oppressor revealed as Satan, who deploys his demonic hordes to hinder the human race from embracing truth. In the original text, Isaiah wrote that those who are liberated become "oaks of righteousness, a planting of the Lord for the display of his splendor" (Is 61:3b). Isaiah's word picture captures the beauty of discipleship: a life characterized by deep roots and abundant fruits. This is the Lord's plan for the redeemed person.

OVERTHROWING STRONGHOLDS

Whether we ponder the spiritual state of an individual or wonder about the eternal destiny of the multitudes, we need to see people as Jesus did. Talking with Nicodemus, a respected Sanhedrin leader, the Lord shared a profound insight: "This is the verdict: Light has come into the world, but men loved darkness instead of light because their deeds were evil" (Jn 3:19).

The One who discerns hearts put his finger on the real source of resistance to the good news: humanity's prideful and persistent love of its own ways, a willful rejection of light. Yet to portray men and women as hostages held by the hosts of hell totally against their will does not paint the whole picture. That would be overly simplistic.

Scripture makes clear the pathway of salvation: every person who hears the words of Christ has a choice to receive or reject them. This is true. But we also need to be aware of the dimension of spiritual warfare. The will of God (who seeks the salvation of humankind) squarely conflicts with the will of Satan (who seeks our destruction). Pronouncing the message of Christ crucified in the power of the Holy Spirit becomes imperative if we are to penetrate the veil of darkness and persuade a self-satisfied heart to seek eternal realities.

Jesus continually dealt head-on with strongholds of unbelief, doubt, self-will, and rebellion. What is a stronghold? It is an entrenched pattern of thought, an ideology, value, or behavior that is contrary to the word and will of God. As Paul depicts in 2 Corinthians 10:3-5, the stronghold exists within a person, but is traceable to and exploited by satanic forces. Certain "arguments" and "pretensions" repeatedly rise up against the knowledge of God. "How can you say there is only one way of salvation?" "Jesus was certainly a great teacher, one of many through the centuries." "Everyone knows the Bible is full of discrepancies." "Every person has a right to choose his own path."

A stronghold is an entrenched pattern of thought,
an ideology, value, or behavior that is contrary to
the word and will of God.

Our culture is littered with demonically inspired values and ideologies such as intellectual cynicism, hedonism, greed, racial pride, and hatred. I believe Frank Sinatra's biographical song "I Did It My Way" exposes one of our more glaring cultural strongholds: the idolatry of individualism. Such ways of thinking and living may emanate from the human heart, but they can also be manipulated by satanic forces. We need to wield divine weapons in order to expose and tear down strongholds that are blatantly anti-Christian.

In his first epistle, John comments that "the whole world is under the control of the evil one" (1 Jn 5:19). What does he mean? Are all men, women, and children outside of Jesus Christ demon-possessed? Or is Satan's strategy one of domination at a distance by delegating demonic beings to pollute the human mind?

I reject the notion that every non-Christian person is possessed by a personal spirit, though some surely are. I believe the chief scheme of the arch-deceiver is to control the way people think, to tamper with the very notion of truth, to twist reality to conform to his own evil designs. Satan uses many potential avenues to distort the way things *really* are, such as moral relativism, nontheistic religious systems, ideological causes, human philosophies, the pursuit of secular science, and the hope of salvation through political or economic means.

Unbelievers are hindered by ideas and arguments that keep them from the kingdom. Christians struggle with strongholds of a different sort, things like fear, low self-esteem, doubt, unbelief, and besetting sins. Satan uses these "pressure points" to keep many believers stifled and sidelined. We continually confront voices from the "old man" that undermine confidence in God, diminish the power of his Word, or deceive us from seeing who we are as sons and daughters of the King. Many of these false assertions sound hauntingly familiar: "God doesn't really have my best interests at heart.... I don't think the Lord hears my prayers.... I don't amount to a whole lot in the kingdom."

If you listen to any of these lies or half-truths and then choose to dwell on them, Satan will rob you of the confidence and joy of your inheritance. He's a terrorist and a thief. He wants your good fruit to rot as well. You can break these strongholds by applying the principles contained in this book.

CONSUMED WITH JEALOUSY

It should be obvious that I approach this topic with a major presupposition: I believe Satan is a real, personal, and supernatural agent of evil whose character is contradictory to the Almighty and who opposes the work of redemption. Other authors have focused on proving the reality of the devil and demons. I appeal to you in this book as to those already convinced of the reality of the demonic resistance involved in efforts to bring people into relationship with Christ.

Assuming the existence of a real devil who manages hordes of evil spirits that deceive people, here's the important question: what is Satan's "thing"? What motivates him to be so committed to cunning and cruelty? Understanding this is crucial to engaging in spiritual warfare. Timothy Warner, missions professor at Trinity Evangelical Divinity School, captures the essence of evil in this way: "At some point in the creative process, Lucifer allowed jealousy of God and his glory to possess him until he had an insatiable desire to be like God, if not actually to take God's place."[1]

At the creation of the human race, Satan's jealousy intensified when God placed his affection on a creature made in his own image and likeness. Adam and Eve were trapped in time, subject to the tamperings of the demonic world. Satan wanted the glory for himself. Beneath the jealousy lurked the greater flaw of pride and a craving for power. Warner identifies three stages of jealousy:

1. To want what someone else has.
2. To hate another for having something we know we cannot possess.
3. To do irrational and destructive things to try to deprive another of what he has.

Jealousy in its ugliest form consumes Satan. His motivation in spiritual warfare is to mar the image of God in the lives of the redeemed and to hinder as many as possible from being restored in his image. In view of the potential glory of God manifest in people from every race, tongue, and tribe, the devil employs every means possible to divert people from redemptive truth.

The schemes of the evil one run the gamut from the most blatant degradation to the finest subtlety of deception. At one extreme, he appears boldly as the monster he really is, the object of worship in organized, ritualistic satanism. At the other extreme, Satan "masquerades as an angel of light" (2 Cor 11:14), promoting religious and ideological systems that may look like truth, but in reality deny the atoning sacrifice of Christ.

Satan's motivation in spiritual warfare is to mar the image of God in the lives of the redeemed and to hinder as many others as possible from being restored in his image.

My focus in this book is to promote a more discerning recognition of these demonic schemes, along with a more aggressive practice of spiritual authority. By putting these principles into practice we can increase both the quantity and quality of the harvest with family members, neighbors, colleagues, and personal acquaintances.

How might such an encounter look in everyday life? Let's suppose that you've found a new hairdresser. On the surface, she seems pleasant enough and competent in her job. But in the course of conversation, you start to hear things that spark your attention. This hairdresser chats about her interest in yoga and about learning how to "harmonize the energy flow" in her body. You notice a small sticker on the edge of her mirror: "PLANETARY PEACE THROUGH MEDITATION."

What do you do? Unfortunately, many Christians fail to pick up on these clues. Those who do sometimes fall into a knee-jerk judgment and overreact. As a Christian, should you continue to go to this particular hairdresser? Should you let her care for your daughter's hair? How do you pray protection for your daughter and yourself? What can you do in prayer to expose and weaken enemy activity in this woman's life? This kind of contact is increasing in both frequency and intensity. A post-Christian culture serves as a virtual spawning ground for strongholds.

GIANTS IN THE LAND

Theologians and Bible commentators are touching more frequently on the topic of "territorial spirits." The relevant question can be phrased in this way: "What are these geographical powers of evil and what is the Church to do about them?" A diversity of understanding surrounds the exact identity of these "principalities and powers." Chapter two of my first book, *The Believer's Guide to Spiritual Warfare*, discusses the nature of these principalities.[2] I'll explore this topic in greater depth in chapter seven of this book.

Opinions generally fall into three different camps. Some people say these powers are definite and personal spirit-beings of a high order. Others insist this is merely personified language used to describe the impersonal influence of evil that infects human institutions. A third perspective blends the other two together by suggesting personal beings who subtly infuse demonic deception into natural human affairs.

My own research and experience has led me to land squarely in the third category. While I affirm that such forces are indeed personal agents of evil, I believe their effect on a particular grouping of people may indeed *appear* to be impersonal. My conversations with those involved in the fight against legalized abortion or the proliferation of pornography provides apt descriptions of such demonic activity. Those people often say, "There is something dark and very demonic about this business—I can't get a handle on it, but I know it's supernatural."

They're right. A fine, fuzzy line exists between those who hold anti-Christian values and perspectives and the influence of actual spirits of the antichrist. The fallen powers inject a toxic influence into a culture, evils like deceit, greed, or lust for power. These demonic influences then work to control the thought patterns and actions of the culture. We need to see this reality from a biblical perspective, while at the same time guarding against undue paranoia or fanaticism.

Scripture asserts that the "whole world is under the control of the evil one" (1 Jn 5:19). What does this mean? How does Satan exert control? *By controlling ideologies*—the way people think about life and its meaning. *By influencing values*—those attitudes and activities people count of importance. *By promoting indulgence in carnality*—such as the high from drugs, an illicit sexual stimulus, or the buzz the gambler gets off a slot machine or playing the horses.

But, you may ask, aren't all these things simply base, human behavior? Sure they are. But we need to look beyond the natural in order to see the invisible vapors of spiritual nerve gas that hover around the masses of men and women, poisoning minds with a distorted understanding of reality.

If we truly want our message to be more relevant, we must make a worldview shift to understand spiritual power. After all, Christians are supposed to be guides to the portals of a supernatural kingdom.

In his book on current movements in missions, *The Last of the Giants,* George Otis analyzes our planet from a perspective other than race, language, or nationality. He calls his analytical principle "spiritual mapping," which he defines as "superimposing our understanding of forces and events in the spiritual domain onto places and circumstances in the material world."[3] This new spiritual science already is having profound impact on how we look at missions.

Otis puts his finger directly on the "big three" strongholds in our day: materialism, the militant Islamic movement, and the New Age movement.

Otis puts his finger directly on the "big three" strongholds in our day: materialism, the militant Islamic movement, and the New Age movement. He connects human ideologies with invisible power in a very clear way: "Man inspired initiatives turn quickly into manmade substitutes—idolatrous doorways through which demonic agents access societies and inflict spiritual bondage. Oblivious to these infiltrations, modern man has become prey to the dark side of his own house."[4]

The sudden collapse of communism actually provides a highly advantageous atmosphere for the "big three." In the summer of 1992, I observed firsthand the radical change in the spiritual climate of Hungary and Czechoslovakia. The advent of political freedom has brought enormous opportunity for the gospel. But it has also swung doors wide open for cultic and occultic groups of all sorts to seek converts. The appeal of materialism also rushes in to fill the vacuum of the former poverty.

The recent surge of interest in Islam makes it a major source of spiritual influence in our world today. Even while negotiations for peace grind on, numerous Muslim nations and individual terrorist organizations remain committed to the destruction of Israel. Otis analyzes the current political implications of the rise of Islam in some detail. He theorizes the possible formation of a massive Islamic confederacy stretching from Turkey, through the former Soviet republics, and over into Pakistan. This confederation, he suggests, may be the combined force that Ezekiel foresaw staging an invasion into Northern Israel—now that the fear of the "Russian Bear" is gone.

In light of these shifting winds, what should our strategy be for penetrating Islamic strongholds and leading those held captive into the truth of the gospel? In reality, our world is shrinking fast. Muslims are merging into Western culture in increasing numbers. Many of us will have opportunities to befriend them, build relationships, and pray for them. At the time of this writing, conversions in Muslim nations are steadily increasing.

The New Age stronghold traces its roots to traditional Hinduism. The growing popularity of the New Age movement around the globe signals the reality of a pent-up hunger for spiritual truth. For an explanation of the message or method of the movement,

I refer you to such authors as Douglas Groothuis and Russell Chandler.[5] Many groups—such as the Christian Research Institute or Spiritual Counterfeits Project—provide excellent materials on the cults and the occult. Christians serious about sharing their faith must grasp a basic understanding of New Age thought.

The core of the New Age message clearly echoes the serpent's lies in the garden: "You shall be as gods... you will not die." Proponents enthusiastically embrace the notion that each individual is God and that each enjoys countless reincarnations to realize this divinity. The variety and diversity of spiritual gurus and metaphysical groups seem endless.

Though the New Age movement lacks any centralized leadership or strong spokesman, the potential remains for this to develop. A current and common unifying theme is the worship of "Gaia," mother earth, as a living organism. This attracts the environmentalists for sure but also attracts scientists and social theorists. Looking for the evolutionary shift in the spiritual consciousness of mankind from the age of Pisces into Aquarius, New Age groups are united in their perspective that Jews and Christians do not fit in the new world religious order on the horizon. Whether it be in Moscow, Eastern Europe, Japan, Asia, or Main Street USA, involvement in New Age thought is growing. It is being dressed with intellectual sophistication and scientific appeal. But these are mere coverings for spirits of the antichrist.

Another cancer gnaws at the core of Western culture: organized satanism. So many ritualistic abuse survivors are surfacing in churches and counseling offices that we are forced to ask, "Has this ugly business always been with us or is this a new phenomenon?" Such abuse has always been there, predominantly in other cultures that practice sacrifice and sorcery in order to appease Satan and gain power. Now we find this darkness closer to home, with organized groups in both city and rural areas.

Controversy swirls around the question of how well organized and how widespread these cults really are. In working with severely abused people, separating factual reality from pathological fantasy presents a huge challenge. Pastors, parents, and counselors must be very careful to qualify reports and allegations. But the fact is, more people are actively involved in the "deep things of Satan" than we have suspected previously. And the primary target groups are children and youth.

In many cases, those involved in satanic cults are also entrenched in drug trade, the pornography industry, the movie and entertainment industries, and racial bigotry that espouses hatred for Jews and blacks. The hard core practitioners of darkness, however, methodically abuse and program cult members to promote their own agenda of anarchy and destruction of godly values.

During a special children's outreach scheduled for Saturday afternoon's session of the Billy Graham crusade in Portland, Oregon, one of the intercessors walked out to the "command center," a high-security area located right next to our prayer room and overlooking Portland's Civic Stadium. A man wearing a security badge approached this woman and asked, "Would you pray with me?" Assuming he was a member of the intercessory team, she readily agreed.

This man began, "Would you agree with me that father Satan will claim the lives of his children this afternoon?" The woman turned and fled to the prayer room. When some of our men went to check it out, the infiltrator was gone. Ten thousand people had been projected to attend; thirty-seven thousand kids and parents actually came to the special outreach session, with eleven hundred first-time decisions of children for Jesus Christ. No wonder the devil had mustered his troops!

We no longer have a choice. In the face of blatant darkness, the children of light must rise and take a stand. We cannot allow Satan to target our leaders and churches with demonic curses. We must not allow his wolves to ravage the lives of our young people. May God mobilize an army of intercessors and anointed workers to confront this growing darkness.

This brief analysis of the giants in the land spotlights the fact that cunning spiritual powers operate behind certain ideologies and movements in our world. But it would be a mistake to over-dramatize this point and begin a paranoiac search for the principality lurking behind every movement. Each human being combines complex spiritual, psychological, and physical dynamics that find expression through a diversity of cultural norms. From my own college training in sociology, I know that much of what molds a person's thinking, personal values, and behavior is determined through the socialization process. Indeed, much of what makes any given person "tick" traces to an individual's choices regarding his or her need for food and shelter, as well as sexual and emotional fulfillment.

I am certainly not saying that most people are directly controlled by evil spirits. Neither am I suggesting a mass exorcism to liberate the multitudes. I am saying that in our efforts to bring people into the kingdom of God, we typically underestimate the reality of cunning powers of evil that blind the minds of unbelieving people. My chief interest in this book is to motivate and mobilize you to act in spiritual authority, to help clear away any spiritual clutter that hinders someone from truly hearing the good news of Christ.

BEYOND EINSTEIN

Ministry experiences often change one's thinking and direction. In the early years of Frontline Ministries, I received an invitation by the Navigators to speak at the University Of Oregon. My assignment was to contrast historical, biblical Christianity with New Age metaphysics. I prepared well.

When I arrived at The Albert Einstein Hall of Physics, I could see that the crowd was mixed. Pockets of praying Christians mingled with what looked to be a majority of the curious and interested, and a few obvious proponents of New Age thought. Having been duped into metaphysical meandering in the mid-sixties, I am always eager to expose the philosophical dead-ends of the New Age.

I launched into my lecture by carefully contrasting the difference between Christian and New Age views on the nature of God, the source of authority, the problem of man, the problem of good and evil, and the ultimate purpose of life. As a way to close, I had considered sharing from Peter's message to Cornelius' household recorded in Acts 10:34-43. Nudged by the Holy Spirit, I made the plunge.

I presented Jesus as the "Good News," the universal Lord who alone can bring peace to the heart. I shared how he had power to heal "all who were under the power of the devil." The Spirit's anointing was building as I explained the validation of Jesus' resurrection by numerous witnesses and his command to his followers to testify that he has been "appointed as judge of the living and the dead." I closed by offering an invitation: "everyone who believes in him receives forgiveness of sins through his name."

As I concluded, I noticed verse 44: "While Peter was still speaking these words, the Holy Spirit came on all who heard the message." I thought, "Lord, let's go for it." Glancing over the audience, I prayed silently, "Holy Spirit, come in your power and touch those who are hearing these words. Manifest your presence in this room."

After a brief concluding prayer, students started to drift forward. Off to my left, a red-haired chap was angrily coming at me, threatening physical violence. Fortunately, a steel desk stood between us. Then, oddly, be began shaking his head back and forth and crying: "What's happening? Can you help me?"

I knew something had been stirred up. I probed further. This student named Greg admitted that at the point of my sharing Jesus Christ as Lord, he was overcome by a violent impulse to throw a chair at me to shut me up. Inquiring about his spiritual state, the floodgates opened. He had been heavily involved in Dungeons and Dragons and had recently taken on a new role in the fantasy game. There was the "open door," the contact point for the demonic. Several Navigators and I talked with Greg and gently challenged him to consider Jesus.

Even for those new to spiritual warfare, this manifestation of evil was obvious. The demons continued to scramble and confuse this student's thinking. His questions multiplied. "How can you say that Jesus is the only way of salvation?" "How do I know you aren't the leader of a cult?" "I want to get out of here... just let me go." Knowing they were exposed and caught, the evil spirits did everything they could to divert Greg from making a decision. This young man had been caught in the middle of spiritual warfare. He wanted me to pray for his protection and send him home.

I counseled, "Greg, only Jesus can free you from this. What is your heart telling you to do?" As we prayed for him, he finally looked up and said, "I want Jesus."

Based on this confession, I weakened the demons with authoritative prayer. I then led Greg in a prayer of repentance and renunciation of his occult involvement. He gave his life to Jesus. I commanded the evil spirits to leave and go where Jesus commanded them to go. The next scene was unspeakably joyous. We watched as the gentle presence of the Holy Spirit settled over him. Greg had become a child of light before our eyes. After being discipled by the Navigators, he spent a short-term assignment in Thailand working with Buddhists and those caught in the deceptive web of occultism and New Age thought.

It doesn't get much better than that. Pure joy comes from watching Jesus touch a heart and crush the destructive works of darkness. The Lord is waiting to bear more fruit like Greg through your availability to him as an ambassador anointed with authority and bearing weapons of divine power for the tearing down of strongholds.

Your encounters may not be as dramatic as this. Frankly, most of mine occur in the midst of mundane, daily life. We all live in a hostile spiritual environment. And we all have contact with people caught in the web of the devil's lies. If you're not already an active harvest helper, jump in and join the fight. The stakes are high, the rewards eternal.

2

Breaking Strongholds in Our Own Backyard

COLLEEN IS WIFE AND MOTHER OF THREE who works part-time at a clerical job to help balance the family budget. People admire her as a model Christian woman. She and her family have been in their neighborhood for five years and have steadily built some meaningful relationships with some neighbors.

Now in her early forties, Colleen finds herself bothered by a nagging question, "Does my life have any lasting, eternal value?" Another woman from her church has approached Colleen about starting a daytime Bible study on marriage and parenting as a way to reach out to the neighborhood women. After inviting other Christian women to an initial session for planning and prayer, they feel even more strongly that the idea is timely. They set as their goal to better meet women's needs and to pray for them. Beyond that, they determine to leave the results up to the Lord.

After the initial excitement, Colleen decides not to get involved. Stronger, nagging questions have overtaken her: "How can I be a model to others when I struggle so with my own faith? Lord, I can see you using Cindy, but not me." Colleen's confidence in God and in herself has collapsed. She discovers the reality that though she is a Christian forgiven of her sin, she is not free of the pain of her past. Though she knows God sees her as holy, she is not yet whole.

Victimized by a verbally abusive father in her childhood years, Colleen hears voices in her head that scream "stupid!" and feels uncontrolled emotions that say "worthless!" She has spent years struggling to shake free from these negative tapes from the past. She is angry at herself, angry at her father, and angry at God for not helping her out of this bottomless hole. This vague, floating anger sometimes turns to fury which prompts Colleen to lash out at her kids. She battles against thinking she is overweight when in reality she is not. Colleen, like so many sisters and brothers I have met, wants to serve but is stuck.

Too many Christians sit "on the shelf." Satan uses every means to keep us preoccupied in introspection or stuck in compulsive ruts. We end up enduring lives of quiet defeat, not free to focus on redeeming the unreached. The Christian serious about service must first break free of the devil's wiles.

Let's talk straight about God working in us before he can work more effectively through us.

Jesus said, "I am the vine; you are the branches" (Jn 15:5). Such stunning simplicity is portrayed in this word picture. The life of Jesus flows into an obedient servant, bearing the fruit of changed character and the changed lives of others. But what problem do many of us face? Our branches are crimped, bound by internal, secret burdens. The presence of Jesus and the productivity of his Spirit are blocked. We become anemic branches, not so much in danger of the burn pile, but in dread of bearing no fruit.

God needs to prune us so that his life can flow fully and freely into our hearts. Pruning is painful, but productive. Let's talk straight about God working in us before he can work more effectively *through us.*

"OH THOSE RUINOUS RUTS!"

Have you ever noticed the magnetic quality of Christians who experience peace and joy, those who have found freedom in the Father's love? The one who walks with God attracts others by spiritual qualities much more than physical beauty. I myself was convinced to come to Christ by watching a man whose walk matched his talk.

We must take care not to speak too soon about dealing with enemy strongholds "in others" or "in our community" before we have dealt with our own. As we grow and mature, believers are called to break free from the habits and patterns of the old life. Paul exhorts the Ephesians "to be made new in the attitude of [our] minds; and to put on the new self, created to be like God in true righteousness and holiness" (Eph 4:23-24). The powers of darkness once had their hooks in the habits and ways of thinking of the old life with its many "deceitful desires."

Jessie Penn-Lewis, author of the classic work on spiritual warfare, *War on the Saints,* offers a valuable insight on this war that rages in each one of us:

In the progress of the renewal of the redeemed man, it is to the interest of the forces of evil that any element of the fallen life, whether fleshly or soulish, should be kept active, for as the believer becomes "spiritual," he more and more is united in actual spirit-union with the Lord of Glory, and hence more and more escapes the power of evil spirits, and becomes equipped to recognize them and war against them.[1]

A part of the process of becoming "spiritual" is learning to discern the subtle working of evil forces in our own lives. How have they conditioned us to think, feel, and respond in certain ways?

Paul describes weapons that are divinely powerful and designed to "demolish strongholds... arguments and every pretension that sets itself up against the knowledge of God" (2 Cor 10:4-5). Paul is talking primarily about arguments against or heresies about the Christian faith. But you and I can buy into our own pretensions. Lies. Half-truths. Ways of thinking and feeling that are inconsistent with who we really are in Christ.

On an individual level, I believe Paul is describing such struggles as doubting the truthfulness of God's word, prideful self-righteousness, religiosity, and inferiority. We may fall into the trap of thinking we can please God by our own efforts, only to end up feeling hopeless that we'll never please him at all.

Here we see the two sides of legalism—one side humanly tantalizing, the other tormenting. Neither embraces the liberty of grace. Both are a lie of the devil. One voice presses, "You can do it! Try harder, do more; the Lord will be pleased with your efforts." The other voice whines, "Why bother? The Lord doesn't really value you."

Do these strongholds originate primarily with Satan or in our own fallen human nature? I believe the half-truths, the untruths, and the outright lies that undermine the word of the Lord eventually find their origin in the "father of lies." Satan injected into the minds of the first humans the poisonous power of mistrust, pride, unbelief, self-reliance, and shame in failure.

Self-will is the chief source of strongholds: human beings thinking they know better than their Maker.

What is the most commonly asked question about spiritual warfare? "What's going on inside of me? Is this struggle caused by a demon or is this just my own miserable self?" After many years in deliverance work, I have come to believe that the majority of our struggles trace to the unsanctified self—those parts of us not yet yielded to the Spirit or healed by grace.

A stronghold is not itself a demon. This conclusion is also consistent with insights from James, who depicts a very fuzzy and fine line between the dynamics of the world, the flesh, and the devil (Jas 3:13–4:10). The earthly "wisdom" that spawns the ugliness of "bitter envy and selfish ambition" is "unspiritual, of the devil." Fights and quarrels within the church are not traced *directly* to the devil, but to "desires that battle within you."

Unsubmitted self is the problem: "*You* adulterous people, don't you know that friendship with the world is hatred toward God?"(emphasis mine) Self-will is the chief source of strongholds: human beings thinking they know better than their Maker.

Since such struggles have a tendency to return or resurface, it's not a simple matter of casting out a spirit of doubt or bitterness. James' counsel for dealing with this ugly business makes sense: "Submit *yourselves* then, to God. Resist the devil, and he will flee from you" (Jas 4:7, emphasis mine). Satan will flee when identified as the accuser and the abuser. We can shut the door on supernatural aggravation of our natural vulnerabilities *primarily* by submitting to God and his truth. Resisting Satan's manipulation and exploitation of our selfishness is secondary. When the power of the self is broken, a word will shut the liar's mouth.

I know of no quick-fix deliverances from strongholds. Actually, the human mind seems to thrive on repetition. Increased exposure to the truth forces the issue of submission. Once the distortions of self-elevation or self-abasement are exposed, the power of the enemy is broken and the power of God fills and controls us. In his first epistle, John commends and blesses the "young men, because you are strong, and the word of God lives in you, and you have overcome the evil one" (1 Jn 2:14b). Lies can only live if we choose to believe them. The young believers, strong in faith, recognize their capacity to expose and expel Satan's lies with the single most effective weapon, the truth.

Christians can be theologically secure as sons and daughters of God but still feel miserable in their everyday lives. Colleen found herself in this situation. I'm sure a "spiritual x-ray" of many of my counselees would reveal this same malady. Simply put, strongholds are patterns built into us while we were enslaved to sin and spiritual darkness.

Unrighteous patterns of thought and feeling die hard. Satan seeks to perpetuate and exploit them. These patterns may involve blatant sin, such as lust, anger, fleshly indulgence, envy, and jealousy. Or they may reflect more subtle areas of selfishness like pride and self-righteousness.

James Robison, author and evangelist, shocked his readers years ago with his testimony of deliverance from the power of an evil spirit in his life. His reflection reinforces the perspective of Penn-Lewis: "Satan and his demonic cohorts work to reinforce strongholds that are weakened as the Holy Spirit reproduces the character of Jesus in our lives. The enemy can create diversions to keep us from using our spiritual authority and weapons to destroy them."[2]

If we fail to accurately discern and deal with personal strongholds, we will to some degree allow satanic forces to maintain strategic points of control. When Peter rebuked Jesus for suggesting his imminent suffering, the Master discerner retorted with this remarkable response: "Get behind me, Satan! You are a stumbling block to me; you do not have in mind the things of God, but the things of men" (Mt 16:23).

We all struggle at some level with unbelief, doubt, self-protection, giving way to human foolishness or devilish influence. An increased involvement in Christian service—particularly in prayer, evangelism, or missionary outreach—often turns up the spiritual heat. Predictably, we will feel increased pressure on any areas of our lives that have not been fully surrendered to Christ. Compromise in wrongdoing or failure of character often results.

Anyone who feels led to a stronger role in ministry or evangelism should seriously examine past emotional baggage, dysfunctional family issues, and distorted beliefs. I have seen far too many zealous for missions break down under the weight of unresolved problems. All Christian workers must be challenged to seek greater freedom before stepping into the fire of spiritual warfare.

UNSEEN CORRUPTORS

If we expect to be successful in spreading God's kingdom, we must recognize and deal with the demonic entities which covertly influence the ideologies, values, and lifestyles of our world. The Apostle John warned of the "spirit of the antichrist." This spirit of rebellion is pervasive. It is powerful. It assumes a multitude of forms as John tells us that "even now many antichrists have come" (1 Jn 2:18). It infiltrates and corrupts human culture like an invisible nerve gas that persists in the atmosphere of a war zone.

Chuck Colson recently shared on a radio broadcast about how well his first book was received. *Born Again* was published in 1976. Jimmy Carter admitted to being born again and became elected to the top office in our nation. Christians have experienced a great measure of favor since these events. But the tide seems to be changing. A Gallup poll in 1992 asked people what group they feared most. Fifty percent of those polled responded, "religious fundamentalists."

The time is now to draw a clear, clean line of separation between the kingdom of heaven and the demon-induced values of the world system.

As Christians we suddenly find ourselves swimming upstream. We feel our nation slipping away from a Judeo-Christian consensus. The "pro-self" issues claim top billing: pro-choice on abortion, free choice of sexual preference, strong opinions on militant feminism, children's rights. As I've watched and listened to proponents of these positions, I perceive a persuasive power at work. We fight not merely flesh and blood, but battle against the spirits of many antichrists which use people to espouse ideologies blatantly disobedient to God's revealed truth.

Our one hope of restoring God's favor in our land is to repent of our wicked ways and face these idolatrous strongholds.

The time is now to draw a clear, clean line of separation between the kingdom of heaven and the demon-induced values of the world system.

In post-cold war America, we find ourselves face-to-face with strong principalities. Self promotes the idolatrous pursuit of individual happiness and fulfillment. Greed and covetousness turn people against one another. Indulgence lulls people to sleep by encouraging sensuality, drug abuse, or pornography. Violence and assorted inhumanities dominate our news reporting. Various shades of idolatry pervade secular humanism, New Age thought, and the entertainment industry. This is but a partial list of the spiritual powers of darkness that pervade our nation. We can no longer safely welcome these influences into our family room through television, video recorders, and other media. Christian families must make concerted efforts to teach their children to discern truth from falsehood.

What disturbs me is that these enemy strongholds have backed God's people into a corner. Christians are called to serve our culture as a holy priesthood. Instead we have become apologetic and paltry. The same repetitive warnings issued in Leviticus and Deuteronomy to the old covenant people apply today: don't compromise with pagan culture. Don't be enticed by the gods of this world. Various points of crossover and compromise have opened doors for the demonic rulers of this world system to invade the church. If we are to be effective and vital in our personal witness, if we are to proclaim a message of separation and freedom, we must model freedom.

OVERCOMING PERSONAL STRONGHOLDS

In the previous chapter I defined a stronghold as an entrenched pattern of thought, an ideology, value, or behavior that is contrary to biblical truth and which emanates from human nature. These patterns are then exploitable by satanic forces. I want to address the issue of strongholds in the life of a believer in regard to two specific "pressure points" open to enemy oppression: sin and selfhood.

As faith-filled Christians, many of us still struggle with areas of besetting sin like sexual impurity, fleshly indulgences, anger, jealousy, and pride. We're a people in process. We often go through an unending cycle of stumbling, feeling guilty and remorseful, and then experiencing the conviction of the Holy Spirit that leads to repentance. Whether sincere or half-hearted, repentance results in a new sense of forgiveness. We resolve to live free of the struggle. We feel a fresh hope that something has changed.

Sometimes things *do* change. More often, we wait with dread for the weary cycle to begin all over again. It can feel like dragging around the weight of a ball and chain. These discouraging cycles can be broken by a release of the Spirit's power.

Christians also battle strongholds that relate to selfhood. The second half of the great commandment reads, "Love your neighbor as yourself." The Bible assumes that we love ourselves, and indeed we usually do. But is our notion of self-concept and self-love rooted in God's assessment of personhood? Because of painful life messages and childhood experiences, we may struggle to convince ourselves that we are okay. We may strive to please others and God. These strongholds of the soul can usually be traced to distortions in our understanding of God's infinite love for each one of us.

Perhaps we could pinpoint such struggles as self-pity, perfectionism, self-accusation, or envy—typical traps of the *un*truth of *conditional* love. These struggles cause considerable pain and ill-health in the body of Christ. They rob a child of God of the blessedness of the fruits of his Spirit and render him or her less than effective in the kingdom work.

What's the distinction between besetting sin and struggles with basic identity issues? We can't always separate these issues. One seems to beget the other. The verbal abuse from Colleen's father damaged her personhood and also provoked a deep reactive anger. Let me suggest some directions for dealing with these issues. I am *not* talking about a psychological approach, where we hold out a hope of analyzing and repairing the problem. I am also *not* describing a healing model, in which we expect God to intervene miraculously and fix it.

In seeking a biblical answer, I *am* describing an old school, old style, spiritual model of bringing the struggle to God and submitting the self and its struggle fully to him. Does this sound antiquated? I think not. The power of God is always adequate and available to break such strongholds with the Word, prayer, and obedience.

I do not belong to the anti-psychology camp. Those who agonize over serious emotional or psychological problems should seek the help of a skilled Christian therapist. Do what is necessary to understand the roots of your problem. But I also suggest that you pursue a truth-therapy approach alongside psychological counseling. When a man or woman of faith speaks and prays truth into a wounded or sin-bound heart, divine power is released. It is a power that can heal the root of the problem, and also surround the person with protection from enemy darts.

God can, and sometimes does, deal with these kinds of struggles in miraculous ways. But typically not. We must apply his Word to our own lives in order to discover how our Father helps us grow into freedom. I spoke recently in an inner city church in Los Angeles. My heart ached to see rows and rows of broken people. As I spoke of the hope we have for the breaking of besetting sin and the healing of woundedness, it felt as if the Lord Jesus walked into our midst, touching one person after another. His Spirit planted and watered fresh seeds of hope. Nobody was instantly healed. But God gave grace to those who were processing their pain. And for several who lingered, he gave specific words of wisdom and counsel. This is the ministry of emotional healing.

Purposeful suffering. In presenting this old-school model, I am forced to raise an uncomfortable reality. We all know that the Lord sometimes allows his beloved children to keep their weaknesses for the purpose of learning humility and dependence. It

may involve an inward struggle or else an ou
trial.

Joseph serves as our model here. His ma
meant him evil, wounding him and forever cha
of his life. But the Lord transformed that ev
good. Sometimes trials aren't *supposed* to go away.

The Old Testament figure of Job is the preeminent model of
purposeful pain. After untold agonies, God brought him into a
place of submission and trust. Job's ongoing agony boggles our
natural minds. Emotionally, we don't like it. If we were honest,
most Christians would admit to a secret dread: "Lord, please
don't do the Job thing with *me.*" Yet he might. And sometimes he
does.

Some of the most painful difficulties we face may not always
be fixable. And it doesn't mean God is any less loving. His ways
of molding us into dependent children, however, escapes our
human reason. A young man in my own church suffers from an
undiagnosed illness. I find it hard to see him in pain. I don't
understand it. But he has learned to praise God in his pain and
grow through the adversity.

Paul walked the same path. He speaks of a "thorn," an area of
weakness and struggle that was so agonizing that he pleaded several times for God to deal with it (2 Cor 12:1-10). A demonic
spirit further aggravated and exploited Paul's struggle. We don't
know what this thorn really was. It could have been a physical
infirmity or a psychological weakness. Some have thought it
might have been the painful rejection of his apostleship by
others.

Lord, this isn't right, we think. But when Paul finally submitted
himself fully to the Lord, he understood the purposefulness of
his suffering: "That is why, for Christ's sake, I delight in weaknesses, in insults, in hardships, in persecutions, in difficulties.
For when I am weak, then I am strong" (2 Cor 12:10). Paul's
ability to bear these things and still believe in the Lord's goodness brought God glory that far surpasses our understanding.

God is pleased when we choose to trust him in our pain and

plexity. The hard question is this: How do I distinguish problems in my life that are *purposeful* and *productive* from those that
unnecessarily rob me of abundant life in Christ and hinder my
service? We must each inquire of the Lord for his answer on this
matter. But of this we can be sure—the Lord always wills that we
find freedom from the power of sin, that we find out who we
really are in him and experience the full joy of our inheritance.

Tormenting strongholds are to be exposed and torn down as
contrary to God's truth. But certain constitutional weaknesses—
such as depression, physical illness, or learning disabilities—may
remain. In the murky waters of besetting sins and self, we can
wield divinely empowered weapons of warfare to find victory. By
bringing one's self to the cross time and again, we discover areas
of weakness that must be cleansed and controlled by God's
Spirit.

One goal of this process is *holiness.* God calls us to be holy as
he is holy. Yet personal sanctification is a lifelong process, with
definable points of victory along the way. The other goal of this
process is *wholeness,* the healing work of believing and living in
the truth. This too is an ongoing process, a significant part of
which involves identifying and breaking strongholds.

I share this particular package with the exhortation
to "just do it!" Pick up the weapons and use them
on a continuing basis.

PATHWAYS TO FREEDOM

We have all experienced the tremendous gap between knowing and doing. The strategy that follows is nothing terribly new.
No new truth can be found under the sun anyway. Just new pack-
ages.

I share this particular package with the exhortation to "just do
it!" Pick up the weapons and use them on a continuing basis.

I'm convinced this is what Paul meant in his exhortation to the Philippian church: "Whatever you have learned or received or heard from me, or seen in me—put it into practice. And the God of peace will be with you" (Phil 4:9).

Regularly employ weapons of the Word and prayer in your struggle against personal strongholds. God promises to be present with the person seeking to walk in his ways. I have seen his faithfulness proven true time and again in my own life and in others as well. But let's not underestimate the resistance of the demonic hordes whose purpose is to paralyze our efforts to pray with power. They don't want us to discover the awesome power of the "keys of the kingdom," bold authority in the name of Jesus! You should put this strategy into practice while recognizing the pressures that hinder the process of attaining freedom.

Perhaps outlining the problems would be helpful before we proceed. Strongholds are bound up with our fallen nature and pre-conversion experience; we can picture the difficulties in this way:

OLD SELF
"former way of life"
Eph 4:22

↙   ↘

SIN ISSUES	IDENTITY ISSUES
Attitudes, habits, besetting sins	Distorted concept of self and others
↓	↓
The enemy entices the Christian into sin. Exploits, compromises, and accuses him.	Satan aggravates low self-esteem and takes advantage of unresolved relationships.

With this picture in mind, let's look at how to identify and overcome the typical struggles related to these issues.

LEARN HOW TO DISCERN STRONGHOLDS

Honestly ask yourself these questions:

- Do I see any attitudes, habits, or behaviors in my life that create ongoing cycles of defeat and seem to be avenues for enemy influence?
- Do I wrestle with distorted messages (negative self-talk) concerning my identity and personal value?
- Do I struggle with believing and receiving the Lord's love?
- Do I experience uncontrolled feelings of envy, intimidation, fear, anger, criticism, etc., toward others?

If you can say yes to any of these probing questions, you are probably dealing with areas originally conditioned by "the old life," strongholds of the self not yet submitted and sanctified. Such areas make ready targets for the enemy. A stronghold will be doggedly persistent. It cannot be subdued by reason. It just doesn't work to tell yourself, "I'm a Christian. I shouldn't really be struggling with this."

If a parent, friend, spouse, or life itself has somehow demeaned your God-given worth, that message is bound up within you. We often harbor unconscious, miserable mindsets and feelings associated with that reality. These various "ego states," whether positive or negative, float beneath the surface. They are not only irrational; they are uncontrollable.

For example, it is next to impossible to stop myself from feeling inferior and envious when I'm around a person who threatens me. Or consider a man who was exposed to pornography in pre-adolescence, raised by a father bound by lust. The power of impurity burned into this man's sensual circuits will simply not respond to good reason or strong will. A bondage exists in this area, originating in human reality and exploitable by evil spirits.

I recall a pastor who came to me, desperate to be free of his cycle of defeat over lust. He had read all the books, prayed harder, believed stronger, and even shared the burden with his wife. Yet he still felt enticed to peruse magazines looking for lewd photographs. His visit to my office proved to be the turning point, an "altar of remembrance."

After he had renounced his sin with sincere resolve, I prayed with authority: *Lord Jesus, in the power of your name, release your purity into my brother's mind. Holy Spirit, break the bondage of lust, and close the door on the enemy's influence.* Something happened. This man didn't become a monk. He wasn't freed from all temptation. But a fresh power of self-control was released into his life.

The powerful pain of rejection often presents an additional barrier. A child may have grown up in the midst of a very negative environment. Such ugly realities as verbal and sexual abuse, abandonment by parents, emotional traumas, and dysfunctional homes often create a burdened existence. The weight of the pain can become enormous—like having to move a mountain every day.

———

Where is God when we feel like we need him the most?
In the face of such ongoing pain, God may seem uncaring—
or else why wouldn't he come and rescue us
from our misery? We buy the lie.

———

Consider the case of a young girl who becomes a ward of the court because of physical abuse. Besides the original pain of abuse and rejection by her parents, she may continue to suffer the effects of being bounced around to various foster homes. Such ongoing confusion often makes it very difficult to believe there is a God who really does care.

The father of lies knows our pain and takes full advantage of this kind of situation. We often experience constant reminders of our inferiority, our need to perform, or our basic lack of worth. Where is God when we feel like we need him the most? In the face of such ongoing pain, God may seem uncaring—or else why wouldn't he come and rescue us from our misery? We buy the lie.

Take time to analyze your self-talk. Do you accept yourself in the Father's love and extend that acceptance freely to others? Or do you feel intimidated and weak around some people? Do you react intensely to others with envy or criticism? Does anger or lust hold a peculiar power over you? Objectify such strongholds by writing them down. (Sample statements might be: "The Lord doesn't really favor me." "I will never conquer this struggle with sensuality." "I'm such a jerk that I quake whenever I see the boss coming.") Such statements are contrary to the Word and will of God. I can't choose to change these thoughts and feelings, but when I choose to trust and submit to the Lord and his truth, he changes them over time.

SUBMIT YOURSELF TO GOD

The old-school approach of holiness as the pathway to victorious living is so simple and straightforward. "Forsake yourself, and submit to God." That statement sounds so harsh, and often is. And yet the fullness of the Father's love, when believed and received, is sufficient to heal us. This biblical simplicity helps us find light on the path. James shares a principle found all through Scripture: "'God opposes the proud but gives grace to the humble.' Submit yourselves, then, to God. Resist the devil, and he will flee from you" (Jas 4:6-7).

God desires to have spiritual fellowship with us. He is waiting for us to want him alone and to find satisfaction in his presence. He grieves over our busy-ness, our idolatries, our human achievements. *"He gives grace to the humble."* If we are willing to be stripped of self and come to him in consecration, change will come, his grace will bring growth in Christlikeness, be it ever so seemingly slow.

Submitting ourselves—including all our hopes, fears, needs, and dreams—to an invisible, transcendant being is not easy. God may sometimes seem obscure, sometimes quiet, and oftentimes withdrawn, but I have found that such abandonment becomes easier as our trust in him deepens.

In my own ministry in numerous cultures, I have found that many Christians struggle with a distorted image of God. The sheer weight of painful life experiences pulls our thoughts and emotions away from trust. Deep strongholds argue, "God is not really good... he doesn't care personally about me... he won't come through for me." The weight of God's Word must counter-balance the weight of such distortions.

Through Jesus, God has revealed himself as a merciful, compassionate Father who always seeks our very best. As you face strongholds in your own life that sometimes seem like immovable mountains, I suggest you take an occasional walk in the woods, or along the beach, or through a park, and honestly pour out your perplexity and pain to the one who cares for you. God gives grace to the heart that is humble. Submit yourself to the Master Potter, and trust how he chooses to place you on the wheel.

REAFFIRM THE TRUTH

As Christians we need to believe that God's truth, rightly understood and applied, is adequate for living life to the full. While all the many psychotherapies and self-help approaches may aid our progress, the living Word is still the key to change. Transforming power is available as we align ourselves with God's perfect plan. In offering ourselves to God, we turn from the conformity of the world system in order to be transformed "by the renewing of [the] mind" (Rom 12:1-2).

When problems never seem to change, discouragement and frustration begin to set in. Focusing on the Scriptures results in a release of grace to provide that extra push you need to get going. In this process of breaking strongholds, "camp out" on portions of the Word that speak truth to your soul. Verbally affirm truth as being what is "really real," apart from the deceptive impulses of your emotions.

I have personally drawn great strength and growth from Psalm 119:25-32, Psalm 27:7-10, and Romans 8:28-39. An excellent passage for regular meditation is from Paul's letter to the Ephesians:

> For this reason I kneel before the Father, from whom his whole family in heaven and on earth derives its name. I pray that out of his glorious riches he may strengthen you with power through his Spirit in your inner being, so that Christ may dwell in your hearts through faith. And I pray that you, being rooted and established in love, may have power, together with all the saints, to grasp how wide and long and high and deep is the love of Christ, and to know this love that surpasses knowledge—that you may be filled to the measure of all the fullness of God. **Eph 3:14-19**

Ask the Shepherd of your soul to make his love personal and real to you. As you reflect on truth, invite the Holy Spirit to apply it to you with his power. Believe that he will initiate the change you need. Pour out your heart to God in private times of devotion. Seek him in prayer with trusted friends, counselors, or in prayer groups.

I recall a season of intense ministry when I became very weary. I took my family to the Oregon coast for a little rest, only to find myself overwhelmed by an oppressive confusion. I felt plagued with self-doubt, doubts about my calling, anxiety about the future. I just couldn't pull myself out of it, no matter how hard I tried.

When we become overly fatigued or stressed, our emotions can spin out of control. I'm also convinced that demonic forces take their shots with arrows of doubt, fear, mistrust of God, and enticement into sin. Mustering the gusto to rebuke a spiritual attack can be very difficult.

On this particular vacation, I arose early and sat at water's edge at sunrise. The first day I poured out my heart, sharing my sense of heaviness with the Lord. My eyes came to rest on one verse in the Psalms: "I am laid low in the dust; preserve my life according to your word" (Ps 119:25). I lingered there awhile, letting that prayer soak into my soul. Then I went on to verse 28: "My soul is weary with sorrow; strengthen me according to your word." The psalmist's words described exactly how I felt, sitting there in the sand, feeling quite alone and devoid of the Lord's peace. I uttered a simple prayer: "Lord, strengthen me according to your word."

The next day I replayed the same scene and sent up the same prayer. On the third day, same scene, same prayer, but this time I experienced a quiet visitation, a perceptible outpouring of God's presence. My confusion lifted, my heart was at peace. I felt "strengthened" deep down where it matters most. *God gives grace to the humble.* I'll never forget the renewing, hope-giving power the Word of God released into my spirit in those days. I was able to return to kingdom-building with fresh love and vigor.

We need to be receptive to the Holy Spirit's work of cleaning up sin in our lives or strengthening our identity in Christ. Take time to simply sit in God's presence. Listen to praise and worship music that draws you into worship. Even if you don't "feel it," develop the practice of praising God and thanking him for what he is doing in you. The Lord will be pleased with your praise (Ps 16:7; Heb 13:15). Rest in the assurance that in due time, he will set you free from strongholds and lead you to greater freedom. Keep *choosing* to believe that all of God's promises are true for *you*, even in the face of discouragement and bouts of unbelief.

TAKE PERSONAL RESPONSIBILITY

Exposing lies and acting on truth releases God's power to transform our character. Admit your denial, lay aside the convenience of blaming others, and face your problem. Whether it is a sin issue or an identity issue, admit that you, in your own wisdom, good intention, and strength, are powerless to change it. The breaking of spiritual strongholds is similar to the first steps of the recovery program of Alcoholics Anonymous. We admit our problem, our powerlessness to deal with it alone, our need for a "higher power" and the importance of human accountability to help shake the habit.

Making such an admission in the presence of another person strengthens our determination to change. For example, the sexual addict may choose a trusted confidant and spill out the awful secret. He or she must repent of both the fact of sinful behavior and the reality of cyclic bondage. The angry father must admit, with a trusted counselor or in a small group, "I have an anger problem." The woman who spreads gossip must openly acknowledge the sin of criticism and malice.

This kind of action can only happen to the extent that a person reaches the bottom of his or her brokenness. A certain level of desperate self-disgust precedes the willingness to confess and repent. But this step marks the beginning of the breaking. Call whatever difficulty you face by its real name, in another person's hearing. Ask for God's forgiveness and help and be willing to be accountable to another person on an ongoing basis.

Use a similar approach when you are dealing with identity issues. You may need to repent of overindulgence in self-pity, envy, or jealousy. Reactive anger, bitterness, and hatred often come with the territory of low self-esteem. But the initial key to victory is to recognize and verbally reject the lies about your identity that have perpetuated a cancer of the soul. Reject those untruths and distorted self-perceptions that are enemies of your growth in Christ.

The Scriptures speak of this resolve in various ways. "Put off your old self" (Eph 4:22); "Demolish arguments and every pretension that sets itself up against the knowledge of God" (2 Cor 10:5). Do this verbally with vigor. Let your spirit speak truth to your mind, will, and emotions. Begin to pray, in new authority, to break the binding power of these false impressions and feelings: *Lord Jesus, in the power of your name, I reject the lies of rejection and worthlessness. I ask you, by the power of your Spirit, to break the power of rejection in my life.*

FORGIVE OTHERS AS GOD HAS FORGIVEN YOU

In order to allow the Lord to fully free you, you must be willing to repent of any bitterness held toward anyone who has wounded or offended you. You need to forgive, that God may forgive you (Mk 11:25). Grudges die hard. But even if you have suffered a terrible injustice, you are still responsible for your own responses to life's cruelty.

Unforgiveness, it seems, is the strongest of the strongholds. It is often a core issue for the Christian who is stagnant or struggling.

During the Nazi occupation of Holland, a remarkable Dutch woman and her family were sent to a concentration camp for hiding Jews in their home. Corrie ten Boom soon came to hate the guard who mocked and sneered at their naked bodies as they were taken to the showers. His leering face seemed forever seared into her memory. Her sister died in the camp, but Corrie survived and vowed never to return to Germany.

When she did return for a speaking engagement many years later, her first talk was on forgiveness. To her horror, there was the same guard sitting in the audience. He could never have recognized Corrie as one of his emaciated, sick, and shorn prisoners. His radiant expression even suggested that he had since been converted. After the talk, the smiling man extended his hand and said, "Ah, dear sister Corrie, isn't it wonderful how God forgives?"

Feeling only intense hatred for this man who had so wronged

her and her family, Corrie ten Boom heard the Lord tell her to put out her hand. "It took all of the years that I had quietly obeyed God in obscurity to do the hardest thing I have ever done in my life. I put out my hand. It was only after my simple act of obedience that I felt something almost like warm oil being poured over me. And with it came the unmistakable message: 'Well done, Corrie. That's how my children behave.' And the hate in my heart was absorbed and gone."

If the bitterness lingers, continue to repent of it daily, and release to God's justice anyone who has offended you. Unforgiveness, it seems, is the strongest of the strongholds. It is often a core issue for the Christian who is stagnant or struggling.

PRAY WITH AUTHORITY

We can analyze our problems, share them with others, and resolve to turn over a new leaf, but the most powerful agent of change is the Holy Spirit moving in reponse to a prayer of authority. Whether we confront strongholds that exist only in the mind or emotions or whether evil spirits are involved, the nature of our praying is the same. Jesus counseled us to have faith in God. "I tell you the truth, if anyone says to this mountain, 'Go, throw yourself into the sea,' and does not doubt in his heart but believes that what he says will happen, it will be done for him" (Mk 11:23).

In Jesus' authority, and according to what he has said about the will of the Father for us, we uproot the lies and tear down the distortions of truth that come from the enemy. When Jesus faced the onslaught of Satan in the wilderness, he simply stood on scriptural truth. As taught and modeled by the Lord, fasting can be a powerful tool for breaking strongholds. Even one day of skipping meals and focusing specifically on one area of need will signal the Lord of your seriousness.

If you're dealing with persistent sin issues, go beyond repentance to *renounce the sin in the authority of Jesus' name*. With identity issues, *forcefully reject lies and accusations.* We need to be aware of negative character traits that can run in a family, perhaps an inherited carnality that works its way down through generations. Characteristics such as prejudice, bitterness, criticism, and jealousy are often learned, picked up by children in early family environments. Such traits can also be accentuated and aggravated by demonic powers.

The truth of God will touch these imperfections at all levels and transform a person into the character of Christ. I am convinced that God simply wants us to learn to take the initiative to employ the weapons he has provided. Don't let the devil stifle or distract you from engaging in spiritual combat. The following prayers may give you some sense of how this kind of prayer might sound:

Pattern prayer for sin strongholds:

Father, I expose to you the anger in my life. I cannot change these reactions. I confess this as sin. Forgive me. Cleanse me. Create in me a new heart, by your power, and renew a right spirit within me. In the name of Jesus, I renounce my rights to my anger. Remove from me, Lord, the root of irritation that keeps this sin alive in me. I reject the thought that I'll never change. Spirit of God, I invite you to cleanse and control the anger in my life. Produce in me the power of self-control and gentleness. Lord, by the power of your Word, I renounce the notion that I'm resigned to being an angry person. Change my heart, O God, in the power of Jesus' name.

Pattern prayer for identity issues:

Lord, you cared enough about me to choose me as your child. I affirm that your love for me is unconditional and unchanging. My own thoughts and feelings are deceptive. I reject the lie of rejection that demeans my personal value and robs me of the joy of my inheritance in your kingdom. I affirm that your plans for my life are for fulfillment and fruitfulness. I speak to the mountains of self-doubt, fear of other people, and inferiority, and break your power over my mind and emotions.

Father, I take refuge in you alone and submit my struggle to you. I resist the accusations of Satan that I don't matter to you and that I don't have a place in your plan. Draw near to me. Heal my wounded heart, speak truth to my inner person, and free me through your love to be available for service to others.

Get tough in taking up truth as a weapon. Keep praying as long as it takes to break mental and emotional strongholds. Don't expect profound, immediate results. You may be at this struggle awhile—actually a lifetime in different areas—but as you regularly invite the Lord into the process, you will notice the intensity of the stronghold diminishing. As you find increased freedom from your own internal battles, you will be more free to focus on praying to penetrate the darkness that surrounds others.

3

Hearing from Heaven

I 'LL NEVER FORGET the night my Lord took time to encourage me, a first-year student at Asbury Seminary. Sitting in the living room, I pushed aside my pile of heavy theology books and began to read God's Word. I felt drawn to John 14 and Jesus' words to his "friends" jumped out at me afresh: "He who loves me will be loved by my Father, and I too will love him and show myself to him" (14:21b).

"Show myself to him...." Jesus, I thought, what does this mean? To what extent can I really come to *know* you personally? The thought captured my attention. My eyes drifted further down the page: "If anyone loves me, he will obey my teaching. My Father will love him, and we will come to him and make our home with him" (14:23). *"Make our home with him?"* I recall thinking, that's pretty close... what does this really mean?

Ever since that September night in 1973, I have been on a personal pilgrimage to discover the experiential reality of these promises. How does Jesus disclose himself to a disciple? How is it that God Almighty dwells with each of us in the intimacy of our inner being?

These powerful promises lead to a simple premise: the Good Shepherd wants to be intimate with you. He wants you to learn his quiet whisperings. He wants to disclose himself to you. Jesus wants to manifest his life fully in those who follow him and pour out his very life through them. And how do we qualify for this privilege? Simply by making ourselves available to him in child-like faith. God certainly uses vessels trained in theological wisdom and those with communication and leadership skills, but he also uses very ordinary people who trust in a covenant-keeping God and take his Word as truth.

The Good Shepherd wants to be intimate with you.
He wants you to learn his quiet whisperings.
He wants to disclose himself to you.

Did it ever occur to you to ask how Jesus knew whom to speak to, whom to heal, whom to deliver from evil spirits? Well, you might say, the Son of God was omniscient—he just *knew* these things! True, but Jesus was also the Son of Man, fully human. John shared an insight into his master that has always intrigued me. Near the beginning of his public ministry, many saw the miraculous signs and began to believe that Jesus was the Messiah. "But Jesus would not entrust himself to them, for he knew all men. *He did not need man's testimony about man, for he knew what was in a man*" (Jn 2:24-25; emphasis mine).

What does this mean? I believe Jesus needed to learn to receive instruction from his Father through the disciplines of prayer. *"He did not need man's testimony..."* Jesus did not need to rely on a psychological profile; he didn't need to check out personal references; he didn't listen to the hearsay and local opinions about certain people. He saw into people's hearts. Jesus modeled a ministry infused with a spiritual sight that enabled him to touch those who were ready to respond to truth.

LORD, HELP MY UNBELIEF

A follower of Jesus can bear lasting fruit in ministering to the needs of others by learning to live in the supernatural. You can do many things for others through your good intentions, but what produces abiding change in other people's lives? The touch of the Master's hand. "Apart from me you can do nothing" (Jn 15:5b).

The Holy Spirit mediates the person and power of Jesus. The measure to which you receive God's fullness depends upon your capacity to believe that his Spirit is waiting to work through you. One stronghold of unbelief that limits your ability to listen to him sounds like this: "God doesn't speak to us today," or "God doesn't speak to *me.*" I challenge you to refuse this wrong notion in Jesus' authority. The Master promised his disciples: "I tell you the truth, anyone who has faith in me will do what I have been doing. He will do even greater things than these...." (Jn 14:12). Do you really believe this? You need to face your own strongholds of unbelief before you see manifestations of his power.

Jesus devoted himself to practicing the spiritual disciplines that sensitized him to his Father's voice. He frequently withdrew to fast and pray (Lk 5:16; 6:12). Jesus modeled dependence and obedience as the guiding principle of ministry: "I tell you the truth, the Son can do nothing by himself; he can do only what he sees his Father doing, because whatever the Father does the Son also does" (Jn 5:19).

You *can* cultivate a listening heart, an ability to perceive the promptings of the Spirit. Do you really believe this? Or does self-doubt overrule that possibility? Jesus enjoyed profound intimacy with the Father. With the help of the Holy Spirit, we can share this intimacy with him (Jn 16:12-15; Rom 8:26).

Sometimes divine guidance comes so simply and spontaneously. Recently we gathered with several other families to enjoy the celebration of a Christian version of the Passover. Months earlier, some women in our church had begun an outreach ministry to international women who were either attending Oregon State University or supporting their husband's study.

This year, there seemed to be a large number of Jewish women, several from Israel. One had already received Jesus as Messiah and had persuaded her husband to do the same—a conversion not typical of Israeli Jews. Others were showing sincere interest in learning more. We invited them to our Passover. We gave them a printed Haggadah that wove together the story of the first Passover with the gospel—that Jesus was the paschal Lamb offered for all sins, for all time.

We all felt the richness of the Lord's presence. At the close of the evening, one of the men took the Jewish Haggadah and started a song familiar to his fellow Jews. Everyone enjoyed this Hebrew-Christian celebration of God's deliverance of Israel from bondage to Egypt and his salvation from the bondage of sin. As we were getting up from the table, my wife, Terri, pursued a prompting from the Lord to encourage Beth, our leader, to give copies of a Christian version of the Passover to each Jewish couple. They graciously took these booklets home.

On Saturday night, Beth attended a local Jewish Seder (Passover meal), where she began talking with one of the women who had come to our "Christianized" version. This woman had taught Old Testament in the Israeli schools. She told Beth she had been studying the Haggadah and had a question: "What does the word 'redeemer' mean? This is unfamiliar to me."

Beth tactfully seized the opportunity to share a deeper understanding of who Jesus is and what he did. Terri was sensitive and simply obedient. The Lord had a plan in mind. He is always looking to involve his servants in the work of redemption. He waits to speak to and use those who have become "other oriented" in kingdom service.

LEARNING TO LISTEN

Just as the forefathers, priests, judges, and prophets were able to receive impressions from God, I am convinced that we too can expect to hear from heaven. Because we have received the Holy Spirit, Paul says we can understand what God has given us. "This is what we speak, not in words taught us by human wisdom but in words taught by the Spirit, expressing spiritual truths in spiritual words" (1 Cor 2:13). Paul goes on to affirm that "we have the mind of Christ" (2:16b). We are "taught by the Spirit" how and what to speak—a learning process that continues for a lifetime. Do you realize the Divine Person present with you at all times wants to impart to you his very thoughts? Such a realization can bring fresh life and challenge to your daily walk as a disciple of Jesus.

This kind of listening can sound subjective, even mystical. I am not talking about revelation on a par with Scripture. The Bible is a complete statement of all we need to know for salvation and godly living. "Hearing from heaven" does not mean that a personal word from God has equal weight with the written Word. Such faulty thinking can lead down the dangerous path of subjectivism. But in ministering to individuals or to groups, the Spirit may manifest his power through a word of wisdom, knowledge, discernment, or prophecy.

Taken to an extreme, this matter of following promptings and impressions can lead to a reckless "God told me" syndrome or a "Thus saith the Lord" judgment spoken about a person or situation.

Such manifestations are certainly revelatory, but we need to be careful not to elevate them to the level of scriptural authority. Who has the authority to say whether such a word is from God or a human being? Any fellowship of believers must be diligent to discern whether words, visions, or promptings are consistent with the Word and ways of the Lord. Personally, I feel very comfortable with expressions like these: "The Lord seems to be saying this," or "I think the Holy Spirit is showing me that we need to repent of our pride." Over years of ministry, people can become proficient in delivering such promptings with both frequency and accuracy.

Of course, if it is taken to an extreme, this matter of following promptings and impressions can lead to a reckless "God told me" syndrome or to a "Thus saith the Lord" judgment spoken about a person or situation. Such impressions can originate from human intention, or can be injected into the mind by a deceiving spirit. We have certainly witnessed such errors and excesses over the years. Sad to say, these faulty leadings have served to discredit the valid leadings that *are* from God and *do* bear fruit.

Speaking in the name of the Lord is no light matter. As a toddler staggers in taking those first steps, let's be careful to take little steps of experimental obedience first. One way to do this is by gently sharing our impressions for verification or critique by others among us who are mature and discerning.

"EXCUSE ME, BUT WOULD YOU PLEASE PICK UP THE PHONE?!"

No one is perfectly sensitive in hearing or immediately obedient in following divine promptings. All God asks is that we be willing and available. I sat at my desk one day, perusing my various paper piles. Feeling a bit pooped, I had resolved to let the phone machine fill in for me. Then the phone rang and I paid no attention. But a thought jumped into my head: *answer this one!*

On the line was a woman calling from Eugene, Oregon, who introduced herself as Sherry. A friend had given her my name and number. Having been a leader in the New Age movement in her area for years, this woman wanted to talk to a Christian who could answer some questions. Due to my hectic travel schedule, I had already closed the door on any further appointments. Another impression came to mind: *Make time for this one!* I set up an appointment.

The day Sherry arrived turned out to be extremely busy. Besides working on a newsletter, I was involved in knotty scheduling decisions. I was preoccupied. Sherry had brought a Christian friend along who sat beside her and prayed. Sherry related her story, highlighting her involvements in metaphysics and occultism. I listened and scratched down a few notes. Admitting to a sense of spiritual emptiness, Sherry described one dead end after another.

I found myself incredibly distracted. My mind wandered every which way. Some of this was normal, physical fatigue. But suddenly I was alerted by the Spirit, "Wake up, she's ready!" I got the message.

"Sherry," I began, "I want to challenge you. I think you're ready to give up the emptiness of New Age thought and give your life to Jesus. In fact, his Spirit prompted me to make this appointment with you. He won't let you down. He's here now, waiting to fill you with hope and the assurance of salvation. Would you like to pray with me?"

Gently sobbing, Sherry repeated several times, "I want to know Jesus... I want to know Jesus." After I explained what Jesus had done for her and read some Scripture verses, she prayed. Her praying friend was bursting with joy as she watched in wonder.

God does such good work—clean, simple, to the point, and effective. Through this experience I learned again the importance of laying aside personal agenda, of living above the weariness and busy-ness of daily duty, and of listening for the voice of the One who knows what is in the hearts of men and women around us. God is the one who seeks and saves the lost, but he will surely use you if you're sensitive to his initiatives.

CAN HE SPEAK TO ME?

At any place, at any time, countless numbers of radio and television waves zip by. With the right receiver, we may adjust the tuner and receive that message. I believe the same reality holds true of God's desire to communicate with us.

The Holy Spirit orchestrates the angelic hosts. He directs the children of light to pray and act according to the will of the Father. If we believe this is so, we can improve our personal tuning mechanism through the practice of spiritual disciplines. I believe the three chief ingredients in learning to hear and heed the voice of God are these:

1. The written Word of God, objective revealed truth
2. The living Spirit of God, the Spirit of truth
3. The counsel and accountability of the Body of Christ as a check and balance.

Charismatic extremism can become overloaded on the side of subjectivism or liberty of spirit. Those who do not take care to filter out what is not of God face the danger of deception through human promptings. Fundamentalism, on the other hand, can rely too heavily on objectivism, the safety of the Scriptures. Those who fall into this imbalance face the danger of quenching the Spirit through theological doctrine and legalism.

A biblical approach involves a careful balancing of God's Word and Spirit. We must accurately interpret and understand the written Scripture as the sure word of revelation, our rock. But we must also be open to the work of the Spirit of truth to illumine our minds to understand and apply this truth (1 Cor 2:12-16). In addition, we also need to be accountable to brothers and sisters in the Body regarding what we believe God is saying.

The revelation and application of God's word to a specific situation happens most clearly in an established community of faith. It is only in this context that we can safely and confidently learn to better hear the voice of God. Let's give ourselves permission to allow God to get through to us, to fulfill his promises. We certainly won't learn without trying.

DOES SATAN INTERFERE?

We underestimate the efforts of the powers of darkness to disrupt or distort our reception of God's guidance. We see this hindrance most clearly in the example of Daniel's twenty-one day fast (Dn 10). High-level satanic princes were hard at work to block communication from the throne of God to the praying, waiting servant. Especially when we begin to pray earnestly for the lost—prayers which may hold eternal destinies in the balance—we must expect satanic forces to counter our efforts by stealing or scattering or scrambling words from heaven.

Do you recall how Jesus warned Peter during the Last Supper about being sifted by Satan (Lk 22:31-34)? Just as the Lord had prophesised, Peter did deny the Lord three times before he turned to strengthen his fellow disciples. How much more do we need to guard *our* minds from demonic deception?

Paul vigorously exhorts the Ephesians to put on the whole armor of God, "that you can take your stand against the schemes" (Eph 6:11). He concludes this crucial instruction on spiritual combat with a call to constant prayer: "pray in the Spirit on all occasions with all kinds of prayers and requests. With this in mind, be alert and always keep on praying for all the saints" (Eph 6:18). All occasions. All kinds of prayers.

One kind of praying is *defensive*, placing about ourselves and others the protection of God's presence in the face of Satan's wiles. I often pray something like this:

Lord, I want to hear only from you during this time. Enable me to hear your voice. Let me know your mind. Father, in the mighty name of Jesus and by the power of his blood, remove from this place any hin - drance of the enemy. Drive away all darkness; shield me from decep - tion. Illumine your truth to my understanding. Stretch out your hand and protect my family from the evil one. Through the power of your name.

Another kind of praying is *offensive*, taking the initiative to thwart satanic diversions. I have found that the one who takes initiative in prayer gains advantage over potential enemy schemes. I continually ask God to clear away satanic static, to restrain the devil's agents from distracting me from following his will.

DELIGHT AND DISCIPLINE HELP
CLEAR AWAY THE STATIC

The interference that comes against this Spirit-to-spirit communion is substantial. We can only hear God if we make him our heart's delight and discipline ourselves to listen for his voice and yield to his will. If we are to see increased effectiveness in our prayer life, we have to turn away from listening to all the competing voices and invite the Holy Spirit to teach us how he speaks to each of us personally.

Let me share two illustrations. In seminary I began reading a classic biography about an intercessor named Rees Howells. I felt both inspired and discouraged by his story. Inspired because of the unique relationship this man shared with the Spirit of God. Discouraged over the seeming unattainability on my part of anything *close* to that which Mr. Howells experienced. I put the book away.

In early 1989, I finished the book. My own walk with the Lord during the intervening years had opened my eyes to the way God uses his prayer warriors to combat evil. The latter chapters of the book describe Howells' prayer battle with the forces of hell mobilized throughout Nazi Germany. In prolonged agony, this simple servant pleaded with God to reach out his sovereign hand and stop Hitler from taking more of Europe. God didn't seem to pay any attention. Hitler kept rolling.

At this juncture the Holy Spirit spoke a clear and simple word to the discouraged intercessor: *"It is not you struggling, but me doing, and you coming to know what I am doing."*[1] Howells found peace with that word and days later was drawn back to prayer. This time he received a clear instruction to pray against the Nazi advance. On that particular day, Hitler made a major blunder and sealed his defeat by the allied forces.

Can you imagine throwing yourself into spiritual combat against such formidable odds? Howells' story helped me to see more clearly than ever that one person's prayer holds inestimable value. And I find no long list of requirements for being used in this way, only delighting in the Lord and obeying his word. God, who alone has sovereign wisdom, knows what he is about. Our task is to learn to listen and agree with purposes that are far higher than ours.

"It is not you struggling, but me doing,
and you coming to know what I am doing."

Another experience showed me God's love and care on a more personal level. Two summers ago we purchased a pair of prescription sunglasses for our son, Joshua, even though I harbored serious doubts about the longevity of this rather expensive item. Sure enough, six weeks later they were gone. After a thorough search had proven futile, I fell prey to normal fatherly frustrations. "Couldn't you have kept better track of them?... You'll pay at least half for the next pair, if there *is* a next pair!... Have you really looked thoroughly enough?" If you're a parent, you know this routine all to well.

Weeks later, while sitting in my bedroom having devotions, the Lord burned this thought into my mind: *the sunglasses are in the van.* In my superior wisdom, of course, I reminded God that we had already looked through the van numerous times.

Okay, okay. I figured I wouldn't hear the end of it until I went to look in the van anyway. I looked everywhere—in, under, above, and around every part of that vehicle. I walked back into the house, nonplussed and wondering whether my impression was mere wishful thinking. Halfway through the family room, I got a mental "flash" of the kid's specs stuck under the driver's seat.

I reversed course, dashed back to the garage, dove into the van, and began digging my fingers into the carpet. Pushing as hard as I could, my fingertips encountered a soft, smooth object. I worked my fingers to the side and slid it out from under the seat. Joshua's glasses case! Few moments in life hold such ecstasy for a middle-aged father. I slipped the precious prize into my pocket and went to find my son. When he reached into my pocket and pulled out his glasses, Joshua beamed with delight.

Yes, it was great to find the lost glasses, but it was glorious to know that the God of endless ages and numberless galaxies took time and effort to tell me precisely where they were! No one can tell me there is not a God who is good and who delights in taking care of his kids!

OPENING THE EYES OF OUR HEARTS

The Holy Spirit may take sovereign initiative with us at any time to reveal a "piece of God's mind." This *impartation from the Spirit* seems to rely heavily on *human intuition* and involves the use of his various gifts. We have the responsibility, however, to correctly understand, interpret, and handle that inspiration by working with the objective clarity of Scripture. This *illumination of the Word* relies more heavily on *human intellect*. As Paul instructs Timothy, "Do your best to present yourself to God as one approved, a workman who does not need to be ashamed and who correctly handles the word of truth" (2 Tm 2:15). When both of these dimensions are working together in the right way, we grow in the ability to consistently know the mind and will of the Lord.

So how can we enhance our ability to hear from God? Paul's phrase about the "eyes of your heart may be enlightened" sounds rather mysterious and mystical (Eph 1:18). *How* does it happen? Consider the following suggestions for learning to hear from heaven.

Come to God with childlike faith. I am convinced that God gets more done through those who simply *take* him at his word than those who spend a lifetime trying to *analyze the meaning* of his word. As Isaiah says, "This is the one I esteem: he who is humble and contrite in spirit, and trembles at my word" (Is 66:2b).

God esteems the person who comes to him in simple faith. Some of us need to renounce our intellectualism, our neatly packaged theologies, and remind ourselves of this profound truth. Andrew Murray captures this childlike faith especially well in speaking about how we should approach God in prayer:

> Before you pray, bow quietly before God, just to remember and realize who He is, how near He is, how certainly He can and will help you. Just be still before Him, and allow His Holy Spirit to awaken and stir up in your soul the childlike disposition of absolute dependence and confident expectation. Wait upon God as a living Being, as the living God who notices you and who is longing to fill you. Wait on God till you know you have met Him; prayer will then become so different.[2]

Abide in the Word. How many of us long so deeply for truth that we regularly feed on Scripture? The distractions are endless. Competition for our attention comes in many forms: activities, television, involvements, social engagements, leisure, media events. Countless good things can at times be enemies of the best thing—soaking in God's promises. Jesus said clearly, "if you remain in me and *my words remain in you*, ask whatever you wish, and it will be given you" (Jn 15:7). Meditating on Scripture allows the Spirit to plant, water, and germinate seeds of truth that will bear fruit in us and in the lives of others.

Paul exhorts us: "Let the word of Christ dwell in you richly..." (Col 3:16). There is no substitute for saturating ourselves in the truth. Be creative in the ways you do this. We keep a flip-pad on our kitchen table with a new verse for each day. We also read the Bible daily as a family and relate it to our everyday lives. I carry Scripture cards with me on my trips and often prop them up below my speedometer. Regularly exposing our minds to truth opens us to the power of God.

Pray and seek God's presence. When you are with a prayer partner or participating in a prayer group, have you ever noticed the observable change when you decide to stop conversing with each other and to start conversing with the Lord? A quiet, holy hush occurs. Prayer plants our feet onto holy ground. Choosing to seek God, to call on his name, meets with his desire to seek us.

How can you make God more the object of your desire? You could begin by identifying with some scriptural prayers, like David's "one thing" in Psalm 27, Jeremiah's declaration (Jer 9:23-24), or Paul's prayer that God would give the Ephesian believers "the Spirit of wisdom and revelation, so that you may know him better" (Eph 1:17). Ask, in faith, for the Lord to make himself known to you, as you make yourself known to him.

Prayer plants our feet onto holy ground.
Choosing to seek God, to call on his name,
meets with his desire to seek us.

Pray with expectancy. How deeply and fervently do we believe that God rewards those who diligently seek him? I believe he eagerly watches for one of his children to venture out on the limb of faith to prove his faithfulness, especially in the face of fear and human inadequacy.

I find comfort in knowing that Moses, Sarah, Gideon, Esther, Jeremiah, Peter, and countless other men and women of God had to contend with the very same fears, doubts, foibles, and flaws as I do. Yet they found faith enough to step ahead into the fray, and walk in the presence of God. Alongside such rising expectancy comes a visitation of the Lord's presence and power.

Listen to the way A.W. Tozer stirs up this element of desire: "There are some, I rejoice to acknowledge, who will not be content with shallow logic. They want to taste, to touch with their hearts, to see with their inner eyes the wonder that is God. I want to encourage this mighty longing after God. Complacency is a deadly foe of all religious growth. *Acute desire must be present or there will be no manifestation of Christ to His people. He waits to be wanted.*"[3]

For anyone seeking a significant breakthrough in this matter of stirring up personal desire, I strongly advise fasting as a sacrifice acceptable and pleasing to the Lord. Set aside a day to abstain from food and seek only his presence. Even if nothing profound or immediate happens, know that God will honor your obedience and respond to the deepest longings of your heart.

Choose to be "other-oriented." I believe the Lord wants other people to be the object of our prayers. That means we must resist the chief natural impulse of self-centeredness. We must learn to put aside our own inclinations and interests and pay special attention to the needs of others. In a tough word, Paul admonishes the Philippians to "... in humility consider others better than yourselves.... Your attitude should be the same as that of Christ Jesus" (Phil 2:3-5).

Self dies hard. But God calls us to choose daily to live in this frame of mind, to become more like himself. He honors and blesses the one who lays aside self for the sake of another. The Lord waits for and wants to answer prayers for "sheep number one hundred." I have learned that if you step out your front door in loving service, God will quietly minister his grace through the back door to meet your own needs. If you want to grow in your interior life, find an avenue of service and pour yourself out for others.

Follow other examples. Every pilgrim needs at least one mentor along the path of spiritual life. In addition to absorbing the written Word of God, we need to seek light and encouragement from other men and women of faith. At various points of struggle and discouragement, God has penetrated my perplexity and put me back on the path by introducing me to another of his chosen seekers. If someone crosses your path in this life who inspires and instructs you, spend time with that brother or sister. Also look for encouragement from brothers and sisters who have gone on before us.

I am consoled to know that St. John of the Cross endured his "dark night of the soul," that Charles Spurgeon suffered with bouts of depression, or that Watchman Nee was violently assaulted by Satan when he wrote *The Spiritual Man.* On numerous occasions, God has brought deep conviction and cleansing to my inner life through Thomas à Kempis' *The Imitation of Christ.* I am now reading for the third time Madame Guyon's *Experiencing the Depths of Jesus Christ,* her treatise on contemplative prayer written from a French dungeon. These books have had an enormous impact on seeking Christians down through the ages.[4]

Tumble in and fumble along. Doesn't this little piece of advice sound encouraging? This tumbling and fumbling may occur gradually over the course of time or hit us in concentrated batches. At some point, in order to experience God's personal presence and power in prayer, we must step into situations beyond our zones of comfort and control. Inevitably we must employ some trial and error.

When we move out beyond predictability, the Lord finds new opportunities to display his glory. But he wants us to choose to trust him. A certain fumbling usually accompanies our first efforts to function in the operation of a gift like discernment, prophecy, healing, or teaching. God may ask us to share the gospel openly with someone. He may ask us to share our testimony or do some teaching.

Take comfort. Every other inadequate saint has likely felt the same way you will feel. Picked on. "Lord, why *me?* Surely there's someone better qualified for this!" Take the leap. Even if it feels awkward and you feel certain you have failed utterly, some good fruit will be produced for God's kingdom. Someone will get blessed by your bunglings! And the Father will get the glory.

Wait on God for a word. In certain circumstances we may find it appropriate and timely to seek God for a clear word—perhaps in making a major, personal decision, undertaking a strategic ministry assignment, or evangelizing someone for whom you have been praying. Learn to come to the heavenly throne and ask. Be willing to offer God the gift of sacrifice by fasting. And for big answers, be willing to wait. Let's admit that this is a huge issue for many of us. Frankly, we need to repent of our impatience and be willing to trust God to speak in his way, and in his time.

I have found no better expression of this kind of hearing from heaven than that of J. Oswald Smith:

> The man who is to be used of the Lord will hear from heaven. God will give him a promise.... It was this divine assurance that enabled the prophets of old to go to the people and declare, "Thus saith the Lord." And until God has so commissioned us, we had better remain on our faces in prayer, lest He say: "Woe to the prophets that run, and I have not sent them!" But when a man has heard from God, then, "though it tarry, wait for it; because it will surely come." And even should years intervene, yet will God fulfill His word.[5]

THE JOY OF OBEDIENCE

Jesus came to touch the sick, the wounded, the hungry. To have any lasting effect, our own spiritual ministry to needy people—whether they be inside or outside the family of faith—must flow from the heart of God. If we want to be used by Jesus in this way, our own hearts must be open to perceive his burdens. And our spiritual ears must be attuned to hear his instructions.

Whether in matters big or small, whether involving nations or individuals, the principle remains the same: *it is not us struggling to do good, but God doing, and us coming to better know what he is doing.* When we are available to him and align ourselves with what he is doing, then God has the option to use us. Then we must leave it in his hands. God will do what he will do. The only question is: who will get the blessing and fulfillment of being the yielded vessel?

God will do what he will do. The only question is: who will get the blessing and fulfillment of being the yielded vessel?

I'll never forget a very special encounter in which God opened my eyes to see what he was doing. Over one hundred and fifty leaders from the former Soviet Union were jammed into a small lecture room in the Ismailov Convention Complex in Moscow. It was October 1990, less than one year before the breakup of the Soviet empire. Close to one thousand church leaders had gathered for a convention sponsored by the Lausanne Committee for World Evangelization. I was invited to lecture on spiritual warfare and evangelism.

My associate, Dr. Ed Murphy, was in the middle of a lecture on spiritual warfare. While standing in the hallway, my attention was drawn to a woman sitting near the back of the room. I noticed a certain intensity about her. Her face was full of fear. I recall thinking, *Lord, is this my imagination?*

I pointed out this woman to a friend standing alongside me and we quietly began to pray. My discernment seemed confirmed as I watched her become increasingly agitated and begin to cry. By this point a thought entered my mind: *I want you to minister to her.* What did God want to do through me?

When Ed's lecture ended, everyone jostled each other leaving the room. Keeping eye contact, I followed this woman's movement into the hallway and stopped her. My friend knew enough Russian to help out. "You are troubled," I began. "The Lord has shown me that he wants to help you. Can I pray with you?" Her name was Victoria. We arranged to meet downstairs in an hour.

An hour later, I began to interview Victoria. Her father was an athiest who had violently forbidden anyone in the family to entertain any religious interest. As a young girl, someone had taken Victoria to an Orthodox church where she sensed the presence of God. As a result of this experience, she had struggled all of her adult life to know him better.

As Victoria spoke, the Holy Spirit gave me discernment about the presence of spirits related to her father's atheism that had been assigned to hinder her commitment to the truth. Her countenance became darker and heavier. By this time, the translation was ineffective. Victoria's friend did not know enough English to help with our efforts to pray. Just then, Olga, an English professor from a university on the Black Sea (whom I had met that morning at breakfast!), sat down alongside Victoria. She asked, "Can I help here?" I assured her she was the closest thing to an angel I had seen in some time and we went to work.

It was a profound time of prayer. Amidst the noise of hundreds of people, I led Victoria in renouncing the sin of her father, resisting his commitment to evil, and inviting Jesus to control her life. The darkness began to dissipate. A quiet but noticeable joy began to bubble up from within her. Victoria was crying, this time with tears of freedom. She was now free to follow Jesus without hindrance from the evil one.

I never cease to be amazed watching God work. No greater fulfillment can be found this side of heaven than being available for assignments that have eternal reward. I encourage you to incline your heart ever more to hear these whisperings of the Spirit. Commit yourself to watch for and to follow through on those divine promptings. God alone can produce fruit that will last forever. Consider the unspeakable joy of meeting someone in eternity who found life in the Son because of your obedience. The following prayer may serve as a guide as you seek to better hear the voice of the Lord:

Lord, with the eyes of my heart, I want to see you more clearly. I incline the ear of my inner person to listen for your words to me. You have promised your Spirit to guide me into all truth and to prompt prayers that please you and bear fruit. Lord, fulfill your promises to your servant. By faith I receive them.

I admit I wrestle with many obstacles—distractions, a mind that wanders, emotions and moods that rise and fall, personal opinions, and a constant battle with busy-ness. Lord, slow me down, lead me into quietness, help me to hear your still small voice that whispers and witnesses to my spirit. Speak to me, Lord Jesus. Help me, Holy Spirit, to separate your thoughts from my thoughts. Show me the person you are wanting to speak to or touch through me. Show me what to pray, what and when to speak, when to serve. Show me your open doors of opportunity. Lord, make me sensitive to you. Cause me to hear and heed your voice. For the cause of your kingdom.

4

From Bootcamp to the Trenches

I REJOICED IN GOD'S GOODNESS as I gazed out the windows of my "upper room" office, located in a building surrounded by oaks and evergreens near my home in Corvallis, Oregon. On this particular day, we had seen the Lord touch the lives of three persons seeking help through the counseling ministry. The phone rang. My wife Terri was calling to ask if I could drop by the local market and pick up a few items for dinner. I headed for town, delighting in the Lord, floating along on some familiar praise choruses. It was a good day.

I cruised into Richey's Market, grabbed a cart, and charted a course down the vegetable aisle. Making a turn, I nearly careened into another cart. I looked up and caught the eyes of an unfamiliar woman. Something different was going on here. The Spirit in me signaled something oppressive about this stranger. I do not intentionally keep my discernment-meter running in public places, but in this case, I perceived a battle being waged over this woman's salvation. I disengaged my cart and shifted into a cordial passing maneuver.

"Catsup," I mused to myself, "that's what we're after here." Continuing on my quest, I began to reach for the catsup when the Spirit of God caught my attention: *pray for her.* I turned, focused my attention on this unfamiliar person, and prayed something like this: *Lord, I lift this woman to you. Pursue her with your presence. In Jesus' name, I claim her for redemption. Lead her to the knowledge of your truth.*

I do not go around looking for evil spirits behind every bush and grocery cart. But God had sovereignly intervened in our collision in the middle of the catsup aisle.

Thank you, Lord, I thought, as I dropped the catsup into my cart and turned toward the dairy section. *Pray again, you're not through.*

What's that, Lord? The prompting was very precise: *pray for her.* I moved back within eye contact and silently prayed some more: *Lord, move in this woman's heart, and by the power of your Spirit weaken the enemy's grip on her life. In your name, I ask you to separate Satan's influence from her mind and stir a desire to seek salvation. Holy Spirit, convict this woman of her sin and her need for a savior and lead her to Jesus.*

Spiritual warfare had been the last thing on my mental shopping list when I had entered the market that day. I do not go around looking for evil spirits behind every bush and grocery cart. But God had sovereignly intervened in our collision in the middle of the catsup aisle. Even though I did not ever see or know the outcome, I felt satisfied to plant some invisible seeds, to wield the sword of the Spirit to free this woman to seek salvation. Only the Lord can measure the meaning and impact of our obedience. Ever since this encounter in the market I have tried to be more sensitive to the Spirit's promptings. I've been learning the power of prayers of penetration, the practice of shaking and breaking others loose from bondage. I have come to better understand my role as an ambassador of the heavenly kingdom, walking through daily life in the anointing of the Spirit, available to pray with discernment and spiritual authority.

Do these things happen only to me? Is this really so weird or is this normal kingdom business? I believe such encounters should happen every day; they should be normal. Any suspicion that such events are weird or untypical tells me that our Western worldview is not in line with supernatural reality. Whoever you are, whatever your role, I encourage you to think differently about your social encounters, to learn some new ways of praying that will greatly please God and put people in touch with his presence.

When Paul appeared before King Agrippa, he recounted his Damascus road experience, one of the most profound personal conversions in history. Paul revealed the word given him from the resurrected Christ: "I am sending you to them to open their eyes and turn them from darkness to light, and from the power of Satan to God, so that they may receive forgiveness of sins and a place among those who are sanctified by faith in me" (Acts 26:17-18).

Paul received this mandate straight from the throne, a personal call to go to the Jews and Gentiles with the gospel. Not many of us will ever rival Paul as a missionary. Not many of us will ever be struck blind by the light of Christ and be restored to sight through the prayer of a believer. But I believe we are all called to share our own personal encounters with Christ with those to whom God sends us. How, practically speaking, did Paul "turn" people from darkness to light, from Satan's power to God's?

We see here a power struggle involving four persons: the Almighty, the ambassador of Christ, the adversary, and the person in need of redemption. Salvation is the sovereign work of God. He acts to send and empower those ambassadors who share his words. While instructing us to "ask the Lord of the harvest to send out workers into his harvest field" (Mt 9:37), God selects some of his messengers to go to specific groupings of people.

But as ambassadors of a kingdom not of this world, we encounter opposition, a counterintelligence that seeks to hinder our efforts. How can we as harvest helpers diminish the strength of the satanic hosts? By the opening of eyes. By enabling those groping in spiritual darkness to see Jesus as he is, unencumbered by caricature and churchianity. By living and proclaiming truth in the power of the Holy Spirit. And by turning the lost back toward the goodness of the Lord. In this chapter, I want to talk practically about the actual doing of this opening and turning. How do we do it?

THE BEARING OF FRUIT

In trying to understand the heart and methodology of an evangelist, I once made a study of Paul's Second Letter to the Corinthians. As I read and reflected, three words settled into my mind: *validation, proclamation,* and *penetration.* Let's discuss these essential ingredients of successful harvesting.

Validation. For the non-Christian searching to find life's meaning, Jesus' message must be made relevant and reliable. This happens only by the grace of the Holy Spirit, whose ministry it is to "convict the world of guilt in regard to sin and righteousness and judgment..." (Jn 16:8).

For anyone to come into the kingdom, the Spirit of Christ himself must touch the spirit of the person. We can pray and ask God to do this, but we must also live the message with such reality that our very lives reflect Jesus, someone who really cares about people. Let's commit ourselves to more readily accept people where they are, appreciating and affirming their value. I like the way Don Posterski describes this: "When acceptance is the attitude and when appreciation for what is good in people is expressed, followers of Jesus are in a position to influence those who have not yet accepted Christ and his teachings.[1]

Proclamation. Paul makes clear that messengers of truth must be people of integrity, so that by "setting forth the truth plainly we commend ourselves to every man's conscience in the sight of God" (2 Cor 4:2). *Commending ourselves to another's conscience* requires that our behavior approximates what we say.

The New Testament offers a consistent model of evangelizing, of presenting truth in a clear and understandable manner. Second Corinthians 5:11-21 sums up our mandate of evangelism. Paul says "we try to persuade men," that "Christ's love compels us" to allow God to make his appeal through us. The language gets stronger: "We implore you on Christ's behalf: Be reconciled to God." Such pleading can only be rooted in a personal conviction that those unreconciled to God will go into an eternal wasteland—a softened euphemism for hell. If you and I are not gripped by the finality of that truth, our proclamation will be sorry at best.

The third ingredient of effective witness involves the realization that an insidious deceiver works behind the scenes of everyday life to sow tares among the wheat and to snuff out the germination of new plants.

Penetration. Up to this point we've been discussing standard evangelism. Nothing profoundly new. But the third ingredient of effective witness involves the realization that an insidious deceiver works behind the scenes of everyday life to sow tares among the wheat and to snuff out the germination of new plants. Paul deals with enemy opposition at one level or another in chapters two, four, six, ten, eleven, and twelve of 2 Corinthians. Let's get past the notion that we are dealing only with human resistance and anti-Christian cultural baggage.

We need time, discernment, and energy to deal with the many impostors that compete with our faith. The false teachings in today's religious marketplace reveal a virtual potpourri of "different Jesuses" and "different spirits" (2 Cor 11:3-4). Aside from the blatant faulty Christology of the New Age movement, we have Christian Science, Mormonism, Unity, and many neo-Gnostic varieties of Christianity available. The angel of light is the master of masquerade.

Recently I caught an evening flight to Los Angeles on my way to Argentina. At the gate before boarding, an older couple caught my attention. I didn't know why. Sure enough, I found myself seated next to Margo, waiting for my "instructions." Through pre-flight chit chat, I learned she was traveling to the funeral of her son-in-law, who was a wealthy businessman and victim of a heart attack.

There are always people around us who need a listening heart and a word of hope. Margo didn't know how to connect with her daughter. After the in-flight snack, she pulled a book out of her bag—a typical New Age self-help book on meditation. I looked over several pages and decided to take a direct approach. "This isn't particularly good reading, Margo." I pulled my travel Bible out and asked, "Have you tried this?"

For the next thirty minutes we talked about the Lord. A divine appointment. Margo had made a commitment to follow Christ three years earlier, but had not settled into a healthy church environment. She had drifted in her faith. To find fresh strength for herself and her daughter in a time of tragedy, she had looked for answers in the wrong place. I opened some of the Psalms to her, and prayed at length for her and her daughter. "Would you teach me to pray like that?" Until touchdown in L.A., we talked of re-commitment, prayer, and the walk of faith.

God equips each of us with divine insight and power to bring down the strongholds of ideas that in any way cast doubt on, demean, or seek to destroy the purity of truth in Jesus Christ.

For the non-believing person, this may take the form of statements like: "Jesus was just one of many great prophets." "I can live my own life, be a good person, and still have the hope of heaven." "The Bible is a great book, a guide for moral living, but is certainly not the Word of God." Relativistic thinking and liberal theology invite strongholds.

SPREADING HIS FRAGRANCE

I am convinced that the *validation* of the gospel is more important these days than the polish of our proclamation or the practice of penetration. God "through us spreads everywhere the fragrance of the knowledge of him" (2 Cor 2:14). This is not just a nice word picture. Our lives should emanate the sweetness of his person. We need to be warm-hearted, loving Christians committed to personal integrity. If we're going to talk about Jesus, we need to act like him.

I'm an avid adherent of friendship-style evangelism, letting an unsaved friend or acquaintance "listen to the music of the gospel before understanding the words." Whether or not they end up making a decision for Christ, most normal people respond positively to those who care and are willing to share. The reality and sincerity of our love is the supreme ingredient for touching the inner core and felt needs of people. Honestly, this is the very heart of my many airplane and train encounters—caring for people.

A recent survey completed in Britain showed conclusively that most converts to Christ made their decision after a conversion process involving significant one-on-one dialogue with a Christian friend.[2] If we love, and follow God's promptings as to when and how to convey the content of the gospel, the Holy Spirit will do the rest.

Dennis Peacocke, a pastor from Santa Rosa, California, hits the nail on the head with humor: "We are the only fishermen in the world that expect the fish to come to the sporting goods store (our churches) and feed on what we say they should eat (a gospel presented in theological terms)! Instead, believers must fish like Jesus did by ascertaining people's perceived needs and catching them on their own food as we lure them towards the boat."[3]

In mixing it up with worldly people, we need to lighten up a bit and exude some human normalcy. Somehow my next door neighbor needs to be able to relate to me and my own life challenges. When I face bouts of bad health, financial uncertainty, difficulties with my children, are my responses seasoned with heavenly grace? How do I respond to crisis? With fear and fretting, or faith? How do I cope with financial pressure? With anxiety or trust in God? How is my neighbor ever to know if I don't talk about such struggles?

I'm not suggesting a super-spiritual approach. No, rather a freedom to be human, to let people see in me a touch of grace that clearly goes beyond the expected human response. Such a response can be tough to pull off in real crisis—a place where the rubber of our faith meets the road of reality. But if we're growing in grace, demonstrating who we are and what we possess, and building relationships with those who don't know Christ, then the Great Shepherd will open opportunities to gather his sheep.

We each have to wrestle with the need to prioritize personal evangelism and work at it, in all of our social contacts in the neighborhood, school, work, athletics, or leisure. We cannot persuade anyone to come to Christ. But the pressure of earthquakes and hurricanes, financial recessions, tragic death, and loss of employment can. That's God's part. We shouldn't necessarily pray for troubles to strike anyone. Life is full of predictable pressure, problems, and crises. And when friends find themselves backed into the corner, depleted of their own resources, and looking for what life is about, the Holy Spirit takes advantage of that opening by sending a harvest helper.

Recently I returned from a ministry assignment in Argentina. I was privileged to hear firsthand the testimony of Cacho Tirao, accomplished world-class guitarist. He shared how as a famous artist, he pridefully felt himself to be a god, able to move and manipulate thousands through his music. All the while his friends prayed that he would find Christ. In 1986, in a freak accident, his own daughter shot and killed Cacho's beloved son. The resulting agony broke him and brought him to Jesus. We can help prepare the soil, but only God can germinate and grow the seeds.

Because it is simply a matter of really loving people whom

God loves, the lifestyle of friendship evangelism is both deeply fulfilling and fruitful. In our discussion of spiritual warfare, let's keep this truth central in our thinking: "Jesus loves me, this I know." As we do, God will increase our commitment to sensitively share that awesome reality with others.

FROM DARKNESS TO LIGHT

Disastrous circumstances can cast innocent victims into a dark abyss without warning, but that does not tell the whole story. By their own choice, people plunge into countless pleasures and projects that promise fulfillment. Jesus said it straight forwardly: "men loved darkness instead of light" (Jn 3:19). Or as Paul put it, we all share a bent to disobey what we know is right (Eph 2:2). We are surrounded by many satisfying things to which we could devote the rest of our lives. "For everything in the world—the cravings of sinful man, the lust of his eyes and the boasting of what he has and does—comes not from the Father but from the world" (1 Jn 2:16). And even though Satan knows how to pull the strings of all this sinful, worldly "stuff," each person can choose to look beyond his or her own failure and emptiness and into the loving eyes of God. Let's come out of our apologetic corners, loving people to Christ on the one hand and fighting against the darkness that blinds them on the other.

We can name and claim and strain in warfare prayer
for a lost soul, but it will not avail unless a seed of faith
is watered in the heart by the Spirit of God.
This is an invisible warfare.

There is no gimmick or Christian magic guaranteed to wrench people out of darkness. The bondages of self-will and unbelief can certainly succeed in shutting out even God himself. We can name and claim and strain in warfare prayer for a lost soul, but it will not avail unless a seed of faith is watered in the heart by the Spirit of God. This is an invisible warfare. It exacts a price. In the contemporary spiritual climate, New Agers and leaders of anti-Christian causes will oppose our perceived evangelical fanaticism with ever greater zeal.

Any servant of Jesus Christ who gets serious about evangelism will likely experience some enemy harassment. We should learn to discern the resistance and to overcome it with authoritative prayer. Attack may come by way of flaming arrows directed at your mind or mood (Eph 6:12; Rv 12:10). You may encounter a "power person," someone energized by demonic forces to oppose your efforts. Paul had to deal with a sorcerer named Elymas (see Acts 13:4-12). You may even be hassled by a local satanist who makes vile phone calls, shows up in a church service, or leaves a skinned animal on your front porch. These days such negative attention is not uncommon.

A conservative Baptist pastor on the Oregon coast stood up to the city council to question the plans of a California-based New Age group to locate a counseling ranch for delinquent youths in his town. The hate mail and phone harassment followed quickly. A local head football coach who is a fervent, witnessing Christian awoke one morning to find a witchcraft pentagram painted on the fifty-yard line of his university's playing field. During the recent Billy Graham crusade in Portland, a young couple on our prayer team were cursed on their way to the stadium. A truckload of local occultists surrounded their car. The leader stood in front of the car, dropping powder from a chalice onto their hood, and muttering incantations.

While you shouldn't waste energy inviting or looking for an enemy attack, neither should you be surprised at anything thrown your way. Praise God for the attention! Such frontal attacks just tell you that you are tromping into enemy territory.

The devil may work more indirectly through religious institutions or government agencies. The seventh chapter of Daniel depicts the kingdoms of earth conspiring against the saints of the Most High. Peter and John faced persistent problems with the Sanhedrin (Acts 4:1-21). As churches begin to develop a plan for more active evangelism, they may begin to experience an internal distraction, like an exploiting of weaknesses in the fellowship (see Acts 5:1-11; 2 Cor 2:11).

Time and time again I have heard pastors tell of extraordinary headaches and hassles involved in trying to secure a simple building permit or permission for additional parking. I don't want to be overly paranoid here, but it seems often that *because* an organization is a church, it may face greater resistance from governmental authorities especially if the church's goal is reaching its city. Why? Because Satan often has his finger in political power. Put on the belt of truth, strap on the shoes of peace, raise the shield of faith, and wield the sword of the Spirit.

Don't get heavy and discouraged. "The one who is in you is greater than the one who is in the world" (1 Jn 4:4). If you prevail in pressing through enemy flack, you'll see the fruit of obedience. Expect trials. Plan ahead to persevere and grow through them. Consider such spiritual attack a compliment!

LEARNING TO SEE THE UNSEEN

Walking in the Spirit involves listening to God in our inward thoughts. But it also involves sensitivity to the spiritual battles raging in the environments of home, office, recreation, and social engagements.

Let's assume that you are in contact with people who don't yet know Christ and you want to add a spiritual warfare awareness to your approach. I would encourage you to recognize the existence of an untapped reservoir of spiritual authority which you can use to weaken demonic influence. Let's learn to perceive our contacts with people with an eye to spiritual realities.

How do you know if someone is being influenced by an evil spirit? You can begin by reflecting on those times when you have made an attempt to share Christ with someone and have encountered an unusually strong resistance. Let's get into the trenches and see how this works. Let me suggest some specific ways to better answer this question.

Cultivate discernment. Some believers are sovereignly gifted by the Holy Spirit to discern the presence of and sometimes even the type of spirit active in someone's life. You can't just decide to do this; it's an endowment, but one which can be cultivated and sharpened. The writer to the Hebrews states that the mature "by constant use have trained themselves to distinguish good from evil" (Heb 5:14).

Some of you will simply be better equipped than others to detect the devil's tampering with a specific individual. But the Holy Spirit indwells every Christian and can guide any person to see the unseen dimensions that influence people (1 Jn 2:20-27). So ask in faith, *Lord Jesus, I want to be a better harvest helper. Enable me to see as you see. Please sharpen my discernment.* Then put up your antenna and tune in! If you desire to receive clearer transmissions and see more consistent manifestation of the Lord's gifts, spend some serious time fasting and asking.

Check for any occult and metaphysical involvement. The Bible makes clear that spiritism, divination, idolatry, consorting with spirits, and astrology are taboo and spiritually dangerous (Lv 20:6-8; Dt 17:1-5). If someone dabbles either frequently or occasionally into supernatural things, a doorway has been opened to darkness. A demonic "residue" may remain that distracts such a person from pursuing truth. These days such influence can come through inappropriate TV watching and movies. Dwelling on occult darkness influences the mind.

If you're building a relationship with someone, you'll pick these things up. The person might ask, "What do you think about ouija boards?" Or, "I hung out with these weird people back in college who did some rituals—what do you think of that kind of thing?" Do some probing. "Have you ever read any books on witchcraft, metaphysics, or occult philosophy, or been involved with any religious groups?" If the answer is affirmative, be careful not to be judgmental. Just carefully ask more questions. In laying a foundation for leading someone to Christ, such conversations serve as good grist for the prayer mill.

Check the family history. After you have gotten to know someone, you should be sensitive to the possibility of occult involvement or sin patterns in his or her family background. Of course you will need to pursue these avenues tactfully and avoid probing without permission.

Overt things will be obvious: satanism, witchcraft, religious cults. Patterns of incest or violent behavior like murder and suicide should also alert you to demonic activity. Keep in mind the possibility of strongholds that may involve habitual human carnality *and* demonic bondage, e.g., violent anger, sexual compulsions, deceit, or chemical dependencies. In many cases such problems can trace either to inherited genetic traits or to spiritual influence.

The powers of darkness seek to enter a family line through the regular practice of idolatry or iniquity. Familial, demonic spirits operate down through generations to strengthen their grip and to perpetuate strongholds. These kinds of spirits will work overtime to keep a sincere family member from seeking Christ. If such a person comes into the kingdom, he or she can still face an upstream swim against a generational demonic current. Discernment and deliverance prayer are required to remove satanic hindrance.

Observe unusual behaviors. Whenever you're sharing truth, watch for any unusual responses, particularly to spiritual initiatives. If the Holy Spirit in you is at work to touch the heart of a particular person in whom evil spirits wield some influence, you can usually see some observable reaction.

Typical manifestations would be heightened hostility toward you, a nervous awkwardness, unreasonable fear, illogical suggestions to cut off conversation or leave the room, a confusion or scattering of thoughts, etc. Look for these kinds of apparent demonic indicators especially when you make any attempt at sharing a testimony, Scripture, or involving the person in prayer. But let me throw in a clear caution on this point. Any of the above reactions can also originate from normal human nervousness. Learn to let God show you which is which and how precisely to respond in prayer. I know of no easy, quick roads to good discernment.

As you follow him, the Lord himself will teach you to better read his inward promptings that will come to you as thoughts, impressions, word pictures, and gentle compulsions.

Kingdom building is a very supernatural process. I can't pretend to offer you any new tricks or methods that promise to enhance your evangelistic success. As you follow him, the Lord himself will teach you to better read his inward promptings that will come to you as thoughts, impressions, word pictures, and gentle compulsions. He will teach you how to better interpret the outward manifestations of spiritual power—whether human or demonic—and how to respond.

Let me illustrate this kind of discernment, first with a case of blatant demonic involvement, then with one more subtle. While involved in some evangelistic preaching in southeast India, we arrived in a very remote, primitive village. I still recall the relief of extracting my cramped body from our vehicle and emerging into the afternoon air. My visit was a mere thirty seconds old when my eyes—both physical and spiritual—came to rest on a woman sitting in the dirt. She was staring at me as well. The suddenness and intensity of her attention were uncomfortable.

Within minutes, we were gathering the new converts to the Lord together for a baptismal procession to the river. This was a joyous time. The music and singing began, while the unconverted Hindus watched with sharp interest. When we began to walk, the woman arose from the dirt and followed the procession.

I knew I had a job to do. After all, I was on assignment. I held back a bit, then slowly came up alongside this woman. An intense battle was building. Her body began to squirm like a serpent and gutteral sounds came from her mouth. Then it turned into a loud hissing. The Lord gave me clear focus and I spoke right out in English:

> *I come here in the authority of the Lord Jesus Christ. I speak now to your spirit and announce to you the Good News of forgiveness in his name. I speak blessing to you in the name of the Father, the Son, and the Holy Spirit. I speak to you demons of darkness and destruction and announce to you the coming of the kingdom of God. The light of Jesus Christ is exposing and weakening your darkness. I claim this life for the glory of the Lord. I weaken your grip on her mind. I subdue you through the power of the blood of Christ. Let go of her. Let go of her.*

As we neared the river, I was still commanding the tormenting spirits, "let go of her." By this point, this woman was in real agony, barely able to walk. Then, to everyone's amazement, after the baptisms were over, she walked to the water's edge and moved out toward the evangelist. Shaking violently, the woman spoke privately to him; then he plunged her into the water.

The next scene will never leave me. When she emerged from the river, I felt compelled to move out to meet her. As I stood and looked into her eyes, violent demons were staring back at me. The evangelist whispered, "This is a spirit of Kali, the Hindu goddess of destruction." The Lord and I went to work and within five minutes, this woman had been delivered of the darkness and brought into the light. Her husband and daughter stood at her side throughout and wept openly for joy to see wife and mother set free from Satan.

That's about as dramatic as it gets. You might be thinking, "I'll never see anything like that!" But these days one can encounter such blatant, unmistakable demonization on the streets of North America or Europe, as well as India. Most of you will never be called to handle something that intense, but you could still learn to discern and deal with many of the lighter cases of demonic influence that will cross your path.

Years ago I began referring some counseling cases to another counselor in Oregon who seemed open to Christian truth and values. Eventually, she began to recognize spiritual oppression in some of her clients and brought them for deliverance. We talked openly about Jesus, the Bible, and the work of the Holy Spirit.

I thought we were speaking the same language until this counselor made the point that all religions in reality were one. I then found out that she was planning a pilgrimage to India to learn how to meditate. Evidently, this woman followed a distinctly different "Jesus."

One day, I gently but straightforwardly drew the line in the spiritual sand and spoke to her about the Jesus of the Bible, the sole source of salvation. She listened cordially, then left. I continue to pray that in due time, the Lord will open her eyes, strip away the deception, and bring her to a knowledge of the truth.

Can we simply open our eyes a bit more to see beyond the natural, to see people as Jesus did? Now that we've stepped into the trenches, let's proceed with specific directions for how to turn people from darkness to light.

5

Helping People Turn from Darkness to Light

W HAT IS THE HIGHEST calling of the Christian while yet on earth? To be an ambassador of the heavenly kingdom. If we take seriously the biblical admonitions about hell, we understand that people are caught between two options: receiving the gift of life or falling into Satan's hands. God's love compels us to draw others to embrace the grace of Jesus Christ.

The Christian who is evangelically alive shines like a beacon in a darkened stadium. Spiritual darkness surrounds us but cannot put out the glow. As the Apostle John writes, "… the darkness is passing and the true light is already shining" (1 Jn 2:8). In the midst of the world's darkness, I believe God will shine through his servants in extraordinary ways in the days to come.

Let's assume you want to shine and let others see your reason for hope. I believe the following suggestions for practicing redemptive prayer will revolutionize your thinking and enable you to reap a greater harvest. I want to help you know how to point people toward the light. I want to cultivate a growing confidence in you that says, "I can do this. I can pray to release the Holy Spirit's power. I can take authority over the enemy on someone's behalf."

PRAY IN ACCORDANCE WITH THE WILL OF GOD

In describing to Nicodemus the work of the Holy Spirit in salvation, Jesus offered a somewhat obscure explanation: "The wind blows wherever it pleases. You hear its sound, but you cannot tell where it comes from or where it is going. So it is with everyone born of the Spirit" (Jn 3:8).

Why does one person say yes to God and another say no? Why does the gospel seem to immediately connect with some people and not others? The Master left this a mystery. A profound interworking of the will of God and the will of man operates here; it eludes the deepest theological and philosophical understanding.

A dear friend and former colleague, Jim Halbert, offered this word of wisdom in a staff meeting one day: "When I enter glory, I'll step up to the door, and over the portal will read, 'Whosoever will, may come.' Then, once through, I'll look back over my shoulder and read, 'Chosen from the foundation of the world.'" That seems to sum up the mystery quite well.

Let's take Paul's word at face value, that God "wants all men to be saved and to come to a knowledge of the truth" (1 Tm 2:4). Peter also affirms that God is "not wanting anyone to perish, but everyone to come to repentance" (2 Pt 3:9). Yet in reality we see many "sons of disobedience" (Eph 2:2) who seem to be traveling the road to hell. Should we see this as proof that our Lord is callous or powerless? No, rather, the evidence of rebellion reveals God's commitment to honor the free choice of those who seek him as the source of life.

The Lord holds out a stirring promise through David to Solomon: "... The Lord searches every heart and understands every motive behind the thoughts. If you seek him, he will be found by you; but if you forsake him, he will reject you forever"

(1 Chr 28:9). We must choose to believe in the fairness of this promise and in the rightness of God's judgments. But let's also be free to admit our perplexity and pain over the unanswered question as to why one receives God and another rejects him.

Grace can seem so cheap today. We present Jesus as the friend of sinners and offer the free gift of eternal life. But what if people aren't convinced of the horrors of hell? We must not deny the biblical assertion that judgment and hell are every bit as real as the current pleasures of this earth.

Prayer is not a foolproof gimmick that guarantees response. In many of my seminars, I talk to agonized women who have been praying for a hard-hearted husband or a wayward child, with no apparent response. Years may pass before that person's resistance has worn down. Recently, a close friend opened up the pain of his own heart over his son's disinterest in anything religious. He shared, "I just struggle to have faith that God will get to him."

Prayer is not a foolproof gimmick that guarantees response. ... we have no guarantee that a stony heart will soften.

We have to accept the inevitable mixing of divine mystery and human will that surpasses our comprehension. In redemptive praying, we must be patient. Yet we can also be precise in asking God to break the will and weaken the influence of the enemy. Even so, we have no guarantee that an individual's stony heart will soften.

I am convinced of the need to claim individual lives for salvation *as directed by the Holy Spirit.* Our Lord is the Master connector, crossing the paths of his servants with seekers in amazing ways. When I faced the emptiness of my own search for meaning in the sixties, the lover of my soul provided a light for me to find my way home. We've all heard numerous accounts of the faithfulness of God.

PRAY FOR CONVICTION OF SIN

I have found that many Christian workers just don't realize how to release the convicting power of the Holy Spirit in another person's life. Jesus explained that "no one can come to me unless the Father who sent me draws him" (Jn 6:44). Surely God can do this sovereignly, but typically he prompts a praying person to ask the Spirit to draw that individual onto a path of spiritual seeking.

We're not talking about a form of Christian "magic" that has power to manipulate people. No, this is the heart of God answering a prayer consistent with his will. God's answer seems to be contingent on the response of each person to revelation. We must also recognize the divinely ordained privilege of the human will to persist in sin (Jn 3:19), and to remain in bondage to the devil's lies (Jn 8:43-44). In the battle for the eternal destiny of souls, we will inevitably grieve over losses. Free will has its price.

How, then, are we to pray effectively? Amidst a multitude of ideologies, pathways to peace, material abundance, scientific and technological achievements, how is anyone to be convinced that his sin separates him from an unseen God and that future judgment is a reality? The task seems monumental, and it is. But we are called to cooperate with the Holy Spirit in a guided, authoritative prayer for unsaved persons.

Here's how I have been led to pray for those who are still groping in unbelief or indifference. (I remind you that the precondition for this kind of praying is an intimate sensitivity to the prompting of the Spirit himself as discussed in chapter two.) I ask the Spirit to cause a *sense of dissatisfaction in the person's heart and to stir a desire to seek the real source of life and meaning.* Basically, I'm asking, "Lord, make this person miserable—back him into an unsolvable life corner, bring a financial setback, personal tragedy, disillusionment with materialism, whatever it takes to stir the desire for higher things."

I also pray for a *softening of the resistance to truth.* This kind of prayer usually needs to be coupled with a willingness to spend time with a person to help clear up disillusionment and misconceptions resulting from prior bad experiences. People today can be touchy and defensive about these issues. "What about those scandalous televangelists?" "If the church is so full of love, why do you Christians argue and split all the time?"

Ouch. Many sincere seekers have been badly burned. Let's make them a long-term labor of love, letting them vent their anger and frustration. And alongside our praying, we need to listen sensitively and reflect an understanding Savior. Reclaiming someone from the jading effect of such caricatures of true discipleship may take years.

I ask, in faith and often in agreement with others, that Jesus would *plant and water seeds of truth in the heart.* I expect God to expose this unbelieving person to the word, since "faith comes from hearing the message, and the message is heard through the word of Christ" (Rom 10:17). In airplanes, dental waiting rooms, during social encounters, I look for opportunities to plant simple seeds and water them with prayer. *Lord, bring into this person's hearing a testimony that reaches him; bring to him some reading material that gets his attention and convinces him of your reality.*

When we see God sovereignly planting seeds, we must pray for the Holy Spirit to faithfully water those seeds to the point of germination into new life through repentance and conversion. You may never see or know the result. You don't need to. Your role is to be obedient to your assignment.

And finally, I have learned to persist in praying that the Lord makes this person *sick of sin and self-effort and convinced of the need for salvation.* This is a gift of grace. Yet we are responsible to keep appropriate pressure on to help persuade a person of the need for Christ.

Some of you might ask, "How bold do we get with these prayers? Do we dare release God's power to break the will through tragedy or trial?" In some cases, a serious shock may be necessary to get someone's attention. Back in my late sixties wanderings, he got *my* attention. Having been arrested for hitchhiking on the New York State thruway, I suddenly found myself languishing in a jail cell in Buffalo. Sensing this was a divinely ordained event, I uttered the reflective prayer of the prodigal son: "Okay God, I get the message."

Sometimes it is imperative that we pray for God's mercy to protect someone from unnecessary danger. *Lord, do what you must do to spare this soul from eternal separation from you… but please be gentle… be merciful.*

PRAY FOR OPEN DOORS

Remember how Paul asks for specific prayer at the close of his remarks on spiritual warfare in Ephesians 6. I believe this is no coincidence. Rather it implies that the work of harvesting is hindered by the powers of hell and can only be effective through earnest prayer. Take care to enlist prayer from others that God would open doors of opportunity for you to share the word with boldness.

Paul asks the Ephesians to pray for his own efforts, "that whenever I open my mouth, words may be given me so that I will fearlessly make known the mystery of the gospel, for which I am an ambassador in chains. Pray that I may declare it fearlessly, as I should" (Eph 6:19-20). The apostle's emphasis on the word "boldly" or "fearlessly" relates not only to the fear of human criticism and rejection but also to the likelihood of satanic resistance. Mobilization of prayer is imperative to move such mountains.

Paul issues a similar challenge to the Colossians: "And pray for us, too, that God may open a door for our message, so that we may proclaim the mystery of Christ…" (Col 4:3). He also asks for prayer that he may "proclaim it clearly." Do you remember to pray faithfully for missionaries and evangelists in this manner? Such redemptive prayer support would result in a much greater harvest for the kingdom.

In praying for open doors, we ourselves have to be convinced of the truth's power to touch and transform lives. Many Scriptures promise that the Word produces results in the human heart, especially light and understanding (Ps 119:130) and faith in Christ (Rom 10:17). Isaiah proclaims that God's word shall not return empty, but shall accomplish whatever he intends (Is 55:11). As workers in his vineyard, I believe we need to ask him for greater faith to expect that the sowing of the seed will in due time produce the desired fruit.

In praying for open doors, we also need to be willing to be the answer to our own prayers. Our pluralistic Western culture has made many of us defensively apologetic about our faith. For fear of imposing our worldview on someone, we may end up walking on ideological eggshells or backing into quiet corners in our conversation. We need to return to the simple, straightforward freedom to share our personal story about how we came to know the Lord even in the face of rejection and outright persecution. Let's remember that John, on the island of Patmos, heard an angel declare that in severe persecution believers overcame Satan "by the blood of the Lamb and *by the word of their testimony* ..." (Rev 12:11).

For fear of imposing our worldview on someone, we may end up walking on ideological eggshells or backing into quiet corners in our conversation. We need to return to the simple, straightforward freedom to share our personal story about how we came to know the Lord.

Paul so boldly testified to Agrippa that the king answered back, "Do you think that in such a short time you can persuade me to be a Christian?" (Acts 26:28). Paul assured Agrippa that he would continue to pray that God would convince him of the truth.

Finally, we have to guard against a pressure to produce results as we pray for people. If we operate on the basis of guilt or human impulse, we'll be miserable and unsuccessful. We can expect opportunities to arise in our day-to-day activities—serving with other mothers on a PTA committee, going to a ballgame with the guys from the neighborhood, mixing with fellow employees.

Does this kind of non-pressured naturalness sound strange? Frankly, this is the only way I can do evangelism! If your heart resonates with his, the Lord will open the doors. Peter challenges us: "Always be prepared to give an answer to everyone who asks you to give the reason for the hope that you have" (1 Pt 3:15a). Caught in the constant press of daily events, we often fail to be sensitive to opportunities to be about the Lord's business.

CONFRONTING THE POWER OF THE ENEMY: FOUR LINES OF OFFENSE

We come now to the practicalities of confronting the work of evil spirits in the lives of the lost. I am convinced that if more Christians put this kind of redemptive prayer into practice, we would see greater results. No one captures better the essence of this kind of spiritual warfare than S.D. Gordon, one of the great lights on intercessory prayer: "Prayer is a spirit force. It has to do wholly with spirit beings and forces. It is an insistent claiming, by a man, an embodied spirit being, down on the contested earth, that the power of Jesus' victory over the great evil-spirit chieftain shall extend to particular lives now under his control."[1]

How many of us believe that it is our rightful role to insistently claim freedom from the evil one on behalf of others? To simplify and understand this style of prayer, let's look at this confrontation on four levels.

The first line of offense: *Spirit-guided intercession.* What do I mean by "Spirit-guided intercession?" Paul's letter to the Romans gives us a partial understanding: "The Spirit helps us in our weakness. We do not know what we ought to pray for, but the Spirit himself intercedes for us with groans that words cannot express" (Rom 8:26). I'm convinced that Paul is not primarily or exclusively referring to the gifting of tongues. I believe these spiritual groans embody the deep redemptive burdens that flow from God's heart into our hearts by the ministry of his Spirit. As we grow in union with Jesus, we increasingly feel what he feels, see the world as he sees it, and pray according to his purposes.

Some believers are specifically called into the prayer closet of intercession. Some will have a particular burden to pray for Christian leaders, others for young people or young families. Some, however, receive special burdens for the lost, perhaps particular individuals or cities. I have known intercessors who feel led to pray for the outpouring of a spirit of conviction and redemption in a certain country or people group. Others pray as prompted for significant world events and are thus engaged in what some have called "history making prayer."

In the dimension of spiritual warfare, some intercessors are led to confront and break the power of territorial evil spirits that hinder people from hearing and embracing the gospel. This is the current practice of the evangelists in Argentina, who prepare with fasting and prayer for their crusades. They prevail in prayer to penetrate the strongholds of darkness in particular regions. Carlos Annacondia, one of the most effective Argentine evangelists, believes it takes a minimum of thirty days of anointed praying and preaching to "open the heavens" over a city. Then the minds and hearts of the people are unhindered, free to embrace the truth.

In the mid-eighties I took a three-week journey to South India to train evangelists in the skills of spiritual warfare. In the home of my host, evangelist Kamalaker, I had requested a genuine Indian curry for lunch. I wanted the real thing. With one cautious mouthful, my entire head was instantly engulfed in a painful conflagration! While trying my best to express appreciation for the meal, my torment was evident to all. Even my polite host and his friends struggled to subdue their amusement.

In the midst of this self-inflicted meltdown, a man walked onto Kamalaker's porch and sat in a corner. He was tall, dressed in tattered clothing, and seemed a bit unsociable. He looked rather odd at first, but especially so when he began to leaf through a well-worn Bible while muttering to himself.

When my incinerated tongue had calmed down enough to allow me to speak, I inquired quietly to my host, "Who is this?"

"Augustine," came the reply. "He prays for India."

This seemed too vague to me, as well as too superspiritual. "What do you mean, he 'prays for India'?" I asked.

Kamalaker explained with a straightforward simplicity. "Augustine left his employment several years ago, feeling burdened for the people of India. He walks from village to village, asking God to visit those places with his presence. Many times Augustine will stay in a village hut and spend hours in the night stretched out on a map of the area, pleading with God to pour out his Spirit. I have seen him do this many times. Augustine agonizes for India."

Suddenly my encounter with the curry seemed insignificant. I felt shamed and inspired in the same moment. Presumptuously, I had thought I knew what "intercession" was. Now that I had met an intercessor, I was scrambling to redefine the term. Surely, I thought at the time, there must be various degrees of this call to intercede. Augustine felt called to carry the burden of God's heart for the entire nation of India. Others are called to carry much smaller burdens according to the Lord's sovereign selection.

I'm convinced that many such individuals are hidden away. They are God's secret, strategic saints, the "watchmen" on the walls of cities and countries who give God no rest until he establishes the presence of his kingdom in a certain city, nation, or people group (see Is 62:6-7). Such watchers are divinely ordained door openers, sovereignly selected to stand and prevail in the strength of heaven against the hordes of hell.

This is the first line of offense, where invisible battles in the heavenlies are initiated and won by the direction of the Spirit of God and with the help of the warrior angels. This is the domain of a Moses, a Daniel, a Nehemiah, a Jeremiah, a Simeon. But let's not make the mistake of elevating only the great lights of the Bible. Countless men and women of simple and secret faith all through the ages, known only to the Father, have prayerfully battled for the manifestation of the mystery of redemption in Jesus Christ.

I am convinced that at this very hour, in preparation for a great world harvest, God is raising his army of secret intercessors to assure the ingathering of a multitude from every nation and people group. In our own homes, we can model to our children and grandchildren a heart for the world by praying for the nations.

The second line of offense: *personal engagement.* If at this point you're grappling with a measure of spiritual inferiority, take heart. You can enter into this next line of offense anywhere, at any time. Every day presents opportunities to bring a touch of heaven to those around us. We can begin to see ourselves as active agents of spiritual authority who are drawn into prayer to command the submission of evil forces to Jesus Christ. When engaged in casual contact or dialogue with the lost, we can cultivate rapport on the personal level while taking an active posture of intercession for the release of God's power.

Dare I share a personal confession here? When I was a kid in Rochester, New York, I would take my magnifying glass out to the sidewalk on a sunny day in search of unsuspecting little creatures. I'd look for some poor ant or sow bug, capture the sun's rays through the magnifying lens, and focus the blazing beam to achieve instant destruction. A fuzzy caterpillar used to smoke the best. Wielding such power over a smaller, weaker creature was a satisfying experience, although it was mixed with an uneasy twinge in my conscience.

But it is precisely this type of power we can wield over the unseen enemies of God, and with no twinge of guilt whatever. While we are building relationships with those who do not know Jesus, we may actively pray in order to focus the beam of God's Spirit so that it pierces the smokescreen of enemy deception.

As I described earlier, I learned in the catsup aisle of Richey's Market that I could act in faith and expect the anointing of the Spirit to silence and subdue the influence of enemy spirits in a person's life. We can allow the Spirit of truth within us to expose and penetrate falsehood (1 Jn 2:20-27). We can focus our prayers in such a way that God releases his light to dispel the darkness that may envelop an unregenerate person.

I'm *not* saying that every non-Christian is influenced by a demon. Some, especially those who have dabbled in the occult world, may very well be. But I *am* saying that in some measure "the whole world is under the control of the evil one" (1 Jn 5:19). In most cases we will not confront the direct work of an evil spirit; more often we will encounter the indirect effects of evil spirits working in our world to condition people's thinking and behavior.

At this level, we outwardly engage a person in normal conversation, while inwardly engaging the enemy with bold authority: "Devil, I expose your darkness in this life and serve you notice that your grip is weakening. I claim this person for salvation in the authority of the Lord Jesus." This has been my experiment now for about five years, and I have witnessed a marked increase in conversions.

We don't get riled enough, in a righteous way,
over the hideousness of Satan's power in people's lives.
Here again, we know we ought to be about battling for souls,
but we get caught in our timidity and apathy.

Evelyn Christenson, author and popular speaker, has practiced this style of evangelistic warfare prayer for years, with tremendous result. Here's her summary of this kind of redemptive praying: "Yes, there is offensive praying for souls that really does produce results. First, we must recognize that all people who haven't accepted Jesus as Saviour and Lord are still in Satan's kingdom and he is tenaciously hanging on to every one of them. Then confront Satan with the power of the *blood* and the *name* of Jesus—and do battle in offensive, attacking prayer."[2]

"Offensive, attacking prayer." Does this sound too strong? not if our hearts are beating with compassion. These are people formed in God's image. Let's love them, but also be bold to loose them from deception. We don't get riled enough, in a righteous way, over the hideousness of Satan's power in people's lives. Here again, we know we *ought* to be about battling for souls, but we get *caught* in our timidity and apathy.

Let me make some additional suggestions. First, *be prepared to offer the person you're praying for a biblical understanding of spiritual battle*, assuming you find some openness for this in your conversation. In short, explain that only two powers exist in the universe, and that people are caught in between. You might say something like this: "Let's realize that there is a force of evil in our world that goes beyond the human level. The Bible reveals the existence of a deceiver, Satan, who seeks to lead people away from God's truth." Share some evidence and illustrations of this reality in today's world. Bring the reality of spiritual conflict to your friend's doorstep.

Second, *for those who have had contact with the occult or who have had occultism in their family history, it is quite appropriate to explain that such activity is considered by the Bible to be idolatry, an open door for satanic influence.* Be careful not to share this simply as your opinion. Open the Scriptures and show your friend the warnings in black and white (Lv 20:6-8; Dt 17:1-5). Allow the authority of the Word to speak for itself.

If familiar spirits are at work in this person's life, the direction of the conversation and the reading of these Scriptures will stir a tension you both will perceive. In some cases, spirits may manifest themselves with such overt reactions as fear, hostility, dizziness, nausea, or a sudden impulse to change the subject or get away from you. If these reactions occur, you know you're touching on issues of warfare. Point out these reactions as evidence of spiritual hindrance.

Third, *be prepared to suggest significant biographies of those who have broken free of Satan's deceptions.* Tailor these suggestions to the person. For example, Chuck Colson's biography, *Born Again,*

may be especially helpful for someone who has looked to pres-
tige and power as a source of meaning. For those wrapped up in
New Age thought, some excellent testimonial books describe the
way out of darkness into the light. For a heavy thinker or philosophy buff, pick up Francis Shaeffer's *Escape from Reason*, or *He Is
There and He Is Not Silent.* Try to find the life story of another
writer who connects with this person's mindset. Then simply
cooperate with the Spirit of God in the process of watering the
seeds.

Fourth, *learn to pray according to the pattern of Jesus.* The Lord
encouraged his disciples to have faith in God so as to cast mountains into the sea (Mk 11:22-25). Pray something like this: "Lord,
I believe, without doubt, that you will remove the mountain of
resistance in Dick's life and bring him to a knowledge of the
truth." Put pressure on the enemy, while patiently loving and listening to your friend. We all need to learn better the fragile balance between love and truth, compassion and confrontation.
Wesley Duewel, an elder statesman in the arena of prayer, says it
so well:

> There is nothing on earth that Satan so fears as prayer....
> Satan is more afraid of your praying than of your pure life or
> zealous witness. Prayer is a militant force that has the poten-
> tial of defeating Satan, destroying his works, and driving him
> out of places and lives he claims for his own. He yields only
> when he is compelled to. You must repeatedly call his bluff,
> reaffirm and insist on Calvary's victory, and force his vacating
> all he has so arrogantly usurped.[3]

When we see someone heading for a Christless eternity, we
have every right to grow bold in our authority over the deceiver.

The third line of offense: *power encounter.* Once you have
reached this level of sharing, you know that you're encountering
enemy resistance and you know your friend knows. Your friend
knows that you know. And you can be sure Satan knows and his
cohorts are nervous. Be assured that *God* also knows exactly what

is going on and has the saving power to pull another life out of the grip of the hostage taker.

If you sense the readiness of your friend to respond to the gospel, then share explicitly from Scripture the message and means of salvation. If you perceive enemy resistance, simply point it out: "Do you sense a tension as we talk about commitment to Jesus Christ? Do you feel any hindrance to your decision?"

If the person with whom you're sharing agrees, pause and bind the powers of the enemy, refusing him the right to influence this decision. But be very sensitive as well to the real issues your friend may have concerning the gospel. There are times for patient prayer and times for pressing a point.

If you clearly sense spiritual warfare being waged over this person's decision, be prepared to expose the sabotage. You may need to address barriers like doubt ("This won't work for me"), fear ("Something bad is going to happen if I do this"), argumentation ("How can you prove Jesus really is the only Savior?"), or hostility ("How do I know I can trust you?"). Keep the focus on the Scriptures, keep appealing to the heart, and gently press the biblical affirmation of Jesus as the sole source of salvation (Acts 4:12).

The fourth line of offense: *decision and confrontation.* As you remain attentive to the Lord's voice, test the readiness of your friend to repent of sin and receive the grace of salvation. You face a significant question at this point in terms of strategy.

- Assuming the possible presence of some measure of satanic resistance, do you lead the person in a deliverance prayer that breaks the darkness and allows entrance of the light?
- Or do you lead the person to Jesus and invite the light of his presence that drives the darkness away?

My own preference is to challenge the person to recognize his or her need for Christ, repent of any known sin, and renounce any doors opened to darkness. Then I usually lead that person in a fairly thorough deliverance prayer, break the demonic ground that allowed the oppression, and command all enemies to leave.

———

When a person is ready to turn from darkness to light,
God's power is present to accommodate the transaction.
And the powers of hell have to leave.

———

You may find it helpful to have this person verbally identify any open doors, points of contact, or relationships that may have invited enemy influence. Instruct your friend to be ready to renounce any ties to darkness, personal or ancestral. Encourage the sharing of a public witness of conversion, like setting a date for baptism, and the destruction of any objects (jewelry, art, clothing) connected in any way to the occult. Share these challenges in the context of James 4:6-10. Then lead your friend in a deliverance prayer similar to the following:

> *Lord, I come to you seeking your favor and mercy. Thank you for leading me into the light. I acknowledge my sin and repent of my rebellion. Lord, forgive me and cleanse me. I renounce my involvement in spiritism, meditation, and divination through the use of crystals.*
>
> *Take away from me all powers that are not of you. I separate myself from Satan and his kingdom. I commit myself to destroy my books and jewelry connected to idolatry. I acknowledge the sin of my ancestors— the practices of witchcraft and divination. I ask you to separate my life from those sins, and free me (and my children) from the consequences of those sins. I renounce the kingdom of darkness, and embrace the kingdom of Jesus Christ.*
>
> *I apply the blood of Jesus Christ now to break all evil curses (be precise here if possible, e.g., incest, hatred, infirmities), spells, rituals, occult dedications, anything of evil that has touched my life. Lord Jesus, deliver me from all evil.*
>
> *By faith, I receive you into my life as Savior and Lord. I relinquish the rights of my life to you and ask for the gift of your Holy Spirit to*

*come into my life as a seal and a witness of my relationship with you.
Lord Jesus, come into my life now and begin to change me into the person you want me to be, by your grace.*

Keep in mind there is nothing magical about the exact words used in such prayers. The issues are sincere readiness and faith. When a person is ready to turn from darkness to light, God's power is present to accommodate the transaction. And the powers of hell have to leave.

SEALING THE DECISION

In cases of heavy occult involvement—personal or ancestral—the devil may reappear soon after such a decision, either out of wrath and anger or to test the staying power of the new convert. I have therefore found it wise to seal the decision.

In any case, we often do new Christians a great disservice by leaving them exposed and vulnerable. In short, we can make assumptions and presume on the staying power of a new believer. In light of the growing intensity of today's spiritual warfare, I strongly encourage sealing the decision by taking the following steps.

Pray for the new Christian. While the need for this step may be obvious, precisely what to pray *for* may not be so clear. First, command the immediate and permanent departure of all evil spirits formerly attached to or attracted to the person's life. Basically, the drift here is, "Buzz off, devil, this is now the blood-bought property of the Lord Jesus."

In this vein, ask for the shielding (Ps 3:3; 91) and strengthening (Jn 17:15; 2 Thes 3:3) presence of the Spirit to surround and abide with the new believer. Ask the Lord to graciously assign and post watching angels to help this new child of the king on his or her way (Heb 1:14).

Second, explain the individual's continuing responsibility to personally resist the enemy: to take a strong stand against evil

(Eph 6:10-18); submit fully to God (Jas 4:6-10); and be alert to future enemy attacks (1 Pt 5:8-9). I recommend Mark Bubeck's book *Overcoming the Adversary* as a manual for maintaining victory.

Third, establish a direction or a plan for this person to grow in discipleship. Don't assume this will somehow just happen. Satan will often concede the conversion, but then masterfully subvert the growth process. Help this new brother or sister plug into a growth environment, whether in a church, para-church or Bible school setting.

Fourth, pray fervently and ask the Lord to guard this person's path and to guide him or her into the fulfillment of walking in the will of God. Pray the Scriptures together here, believing that the Lord will fulfill his promises. (I find these especially helpful: Ps 32:8; 37:3-5; Prv 3:5, 6:2; 2 Thes 1:11-12).

And fifth, simply bless this new believer with the peace and joy of the Spirit. I like to speak Romans 15:13 in a spirit of faith and expectancy: "May the God of hope fill you with all joy and peace as you trust in him, so that you may overflow with hope by the power of the Holy Spirit." Ask in faith for the Holy Spirit to fill and use this person for his purposes.

Just talking about personal evangelism makes many of us feel nervous and evokes feelings of guilt and a sense of failure. All the Lord requires of us is to be honest, compassionate, and available. This is our privilege, not another pressure to perform. Understanding that many people are held hostage to the enemy, we can begin to experience God's heart. As led by his Spirit, we can act in authority to transfer those held against their will out of the dominion of darkness and into the kingdom of light.

When we understand the hidden dimension of spiritual warfare involved in this work, evangelism becomes dynamic, even exhilarating. Our own faith is strengthened by watching the Spirit of God draw a person to Jesus. In the courts of heaven, we will know the blessedness of seeing the fruit of our prayers. With fresh resolve, let's renew our efforts to plunder the enemy's camp.

6

Breaking Strongholds in the Church

JESUS CAME TO DEMONSTRATE the love of God for people and to bring glory to the Father. As his body on earth, the church is called to reflect God's glory as well, to validate and radiate the truth of his words and life to a watching world. Unfortunately, his people on many occasions bring Jesus more grief than glory. I often fear there is more world in the church than there is presence of the church in the world.

The marriage relationship was designed by God to be a sacred trust in which a man and woman enter into a mutual commitment to care for the needs of one other and bring honor to the partner. One mate may say or do something in a social setting that causes deep embarrassment to the other. Beneath an angry reaction, pain often fills the heart of the offended spouse.

One of the more painful forms of breaking trust in marriage happens when one mate brings attention to a flaw or weakness in the other. This sort of public embarrassment may be tactless and unintended, or it may be pre-meditated and malicious.

Obviously, the latter case is more destructive of trust.

In many ways the church as the bride of Christ has been a source of embarrassment to Jesus, her Bridegroom. In his priestly prayer recorded in John 17, Christ made clear that our love for one another and our witness of unity were necessary preconditions for validating his Lordship to a watching, skeptical world. The body of Christ is called to exhibit a purity before God and a unity before humankind that validates it as a supernatural community and the bearer of salvation. Yet how can the world believe what we say until we demonstrate love one for another?

We talked earlier about the priority of dealing with personal strongholds that hinder our freedom in Christ and the strength of our witness. No less important is dealing with strongholds that plague our corporate fellowships. I write in this chapter to the distressed pastor or involved lay person who finds him or herself asking in an embattled church environment, "What really ails us here? Is there more going on than meets my natural eye?" Many Christians remain entrenched in strongholds of pride, self-reliance, unbelief, religiosity, covetousness, sensuality, and idolatry of leisure. I believe such strongholds open the door for demonic powers to accuse and oppress the people of God.

If we are going to see more widespread success in evangelism through the established church we must deal seriously and straightforwardly with the strongholds of sin that weaken her integrity and purity.

Consider the countless people who stumble over the sick state of the church, blaming its hypocrisy. How can we expect anyone to want to join up with a bunch who preach love but secretly snipe at and gripe about each other? How many nominal Christians or non-believers do you know who have been "burned" or "blown away" by a religious group's heavy legalism, a split, strife, backbiting, or the moral failure of a leader? How many do you know who have an embittered tale to tell about "Church Wars"? No wonder so many people are totally turned off. We need to "get real" real quick.

How easy is it to convince these people to step back into a church environment? It is nearly impossible. Disgust and disillusionment take their toll on many would-be believers. If we are going to see more widespread success in evangelism through the established church we must deal seriously and straightforwardly with the strongholds of sin that weaken her integrity and purity. The devil works to discredit and derail the church in its divine mission. But "... the gates of Hades will not prevail...."

Do you feel as sick about this sad state of affairs as I do? Do you feel the grief of Jesus' heart over these issues? No leader or church body will ever be perfect, but I believe we can do a far better job of representing our Lord in public. Let's face the hard task of cleaning up our own backyard. The church is ripe for revival and Jesus never misses an opportunity for purging and purifying his bride. God, help us to recognize our compromises, repent of sin, receive his cleansing, and resist the devil. God, help us to honor Jesus' commands to love one another and to be worthy of his name.

THE PRINCIPLE OF CORPORATE SOLIDARITY

An important principle determines the degree of God's blessing on a particular group: the action of one member of a group does affects the whole; conversely, the decisions and actions of the group are binding for the individual. In other words, God sees the group as one person, knit together as a community of faith committed to his covenantal promises. Let's consider the essence of spiritual communion or community first under the old covenant and then under the new covenant.

The old covenant community. The Lord chose to reveal himself to a particular people. The Hebrew nation was to be his treasured possession and he was to be God to them—an exclusive, covenantal relationship. Motivated by selfless love, the Lord wanted to bless Israel and make them a blessing to the nations.

Time and again—as retold in Exodus, Deuteronomy, and Leviticus—God gave his people a clear choice: choose to love me alone, follow my commandments, forsake the ways of the pagan cultures around you, and I will be in your midst. Conversely, if you choose idolatry, forsake the commandments, and adopt pagan ways, you will be guaranteed two clear consequences: Yahweh will withdraw the blessing of his presence and he will allow a foreign enemy to serve as oppressor. Repentance and return to Yahweh were then the conditions for a restoration of his favor.

You know the rest of the story. Through the period of the judges, the kings, the prophets, and the various exiles, Israel went through countless cycles of rebellion, rejection of God's favor, subjection to an enemy oppressor, repentance, and restoration of favor. In many respects, Israel provides for the church today countless object lessons on how **not** to walk with God. A non-negotiable part of the covenant package requires God's people to reflect the integrity and holiness of God's character. Our violation of this commitment brings grief both to the community and to God.

———

Israel provides for the church today countless object lessons on how not *to walk with God.*

———

I find the incident of Achan's sin especially instructive. Because of this one man's covetousness, "the Lord's anger burned against Israel" (Jos 7:1). When Achan's sin was exposed, he verbally admitted his sin. He was then stoned and "the Lord turned from his fierce anger" (v. 26). Had the sin remained rationalized and hidden, all Israel would have incurred grave consequences. But Joshua acted rightly and courageously to purge the sin from the camp.

The new covenant community. Do we see any parallel conditions of blessing/cursing or favor/disfavor when we look at today's church? "Aren't we living in the age of grace?" one might ask. Does God still require the same level of corporate righteousness? His moral requirements surely have not changed. But because Christ's death on the cross cleanses or atones for all sin, we enjoy greater hope for dealing with sin issues. Further, the Holy Spirit remains actively at work to expose and convict of sin.

Peter quotes Leviticus: "But just as he who called you is holy, so be holy in all you do; for it is written: 'Be holy, because I am holy'" (1 Pt 1:15). I detect no diminishment here of God's expectations in terms of personal righteousness.

Dealing with the issue of separation from pagan culture, Paul quotes Leviticus: "What agreement is there between the temple of God and idols? For we are the temple of the living God. As God has said: 'I will live with them and walk among them, and I will be their God, and they will be my people'" (2 Cor 6:16).

Nothing has essentially changed! The Lord, ceaseless in love, inexhaustible in mercy, seeks a people for the display of his glorious affection. He wants a people who love and care for him so supremely as to honor and represent him in the midst of a corrupt world.

And yet, even in the shadow of the cross, the redeemed community of faith still wrestles with the world, the flesh, and the devil. We always remain free to yield our lives to God as instruments of righteousness or to indulge the old nature. The reality of "sin in the camp" is not exclusive to the old covenant community.

Ananias and Sapphira fell prey to covetousness and deceit. Notice what Peter said to Ananias: "Ananias, how is it that Satan has so filled your heart that you have lied to the Holy Spirit?" (Acts 5:3). Satan constantly seeks points of entry into the community of faith to compromise its holiness and rob it of the glory of God. Paul dealt quickly and harshly with the immoral brother caught in sin at Corinth, reminding his readers that "a little yeast works through the whole batch of dough" (1 Cor 5:6). When this man repented, Paul exhorted the church to forgive him, "in order that Satan might not outwit us" (2 Cor 2:11).

Whether old covenant or new, the principles remain the same. But in light of the cross, the body of Christ is to strive for resolution of the sin through the sinner's confession and the church's forgiveness. Because of the power of the Holy Spirit at work within us, we can choose to be holy and live in the realistic hope of walking in a manner pleasing to God. And when we stumble and fall, the immediacy of God's mercy is extended to us through the atonement.

THE LORD'S DWELLING PLACE

Before we look at discerning and dealing with strongholds in the church, let's look at the picture of the church portrayed in Ephesians. In the first fourteen verses of chapter one, Paul brings to light the fact of God's favor: because he "*has* blessed us" (v. 3); "he *chose* us" (v. 4); "he *made known* to us the mystery of his will" (v. 9); and therefore "we *have* redemption" (v. 7). All of this has happened "for the praise of his glory."

Paul carries a deep prayer burden for this church to experience the presence of Jesus in their personal and corporate lives. He petitions that they would have "wisdom and revelation to know him better" (v. 17), "to know the hope" (v. 18), and "to know his incomparably great power" (v. 19). The apostle labors in prayer that their understanding of Jesus would move from principle to power, from right doctrine to reality.

The Lord still longs to build a visible community which reflects his love and glory. Speaking of Jesus as head over the church, Paul describes this glorious community: "God placed all things under his feet and appointed him to be head over everything for the church, which is his body, the fullness of him who fills everything in every way" (Eph 1:22).

The church is designed and destined to manifest the full glory of the Lord Jesus. "In him [the chief cornerstone] the whole building is joined together and rises to become a holy temple in the Lord" (Eph 2:21). And as if these truths were not profound enough, Paul states that our own bodies, the temples he inhabits, are seated with Christ at the right hand of God in the heavenly realms (2:6).

He speaks passionately about the established reality of Jew and Gentile, slave and free, man and woman, knit together in one redemptive community that has already been "made known to the rulers and authorities in the heavenly realms" (Eph 3:10). This is a glorious picture of what the bride of Christ has potential to be and is going to be in the coming kingdom. But is this anywhere close to picturing the current condition of the church? To what extent are we to accept and accommodate the inevitable gap between the ideal and the real?

David Bryant, one of the leaders of today's prayer movement, boldly believes that we can experience an "approximation of the consummation" of God's glory in the church so majestically depicted by Paul to the Ephesians. Even though perfect holiness may not be typical of the reality of our church life, we can experience a foretaste of the glory of God manifest through the unity of Jesus' body.

We can receive such a foretaste of joy and blessing when gathered with thousands of other believers for united, concerted prayer for awakening in the church. We can and must "make every effort to keep the unity of the Spirit through the bond of peace" (Eph 4:3). God sees only one body, one Spirit, and one Lord who has revealed to us all the one faith.

Whatever God may be doing ultimately, we must take seriously the ugliness of sin and worldliness that have rendered the body sick with the cancer of compromise.

By his own sovereign initiative, the Lord seems to be preparing his people all over the world for a closer approximation of the fullness of Christ. The cross-denominational involvement in prayer and praise, the heightened interest in revival, the cooperative commitment to extend the gospel to unreached peoples—all are signs that God is now infusing us with his presence.

We each hold an important responsibility in this new work. We must be willing to lay aside denominationalism, pride, and self-sufficiency. We need to learn to love and honor one another as brothers and sisters seeking to follow Jesus. Some believe the Lord intends to restore his people to purity and unity before he comes. Some hold great hope that this restoration will be widespread. Others who are less optimistic look for a righteous remnant to rise in the midst of the apathy and apostasy of the organized church.

Whatever God may be doing ultimately, we must take seriously the ugliness of sin and worldliness that have rendered the body of Christ sick with the cancer of compromise. Paul's list of sins at the end of Ephesians 4 are all sins of Christians against Christians! Such sins seriously grieve God and cause him to withdraw his favor and blessing. They also give Satan and his demonic hordes opportunities to gain "footholds" within the church (Eph 4:27).

DEALING WITH STRONGHOLDS IN THE CHURCH

Just as the adversary seeks to gain a foothold of influence in the life of the individual believer, he also tries to gain influence in a church, ministry organization, or missionary endeavor. Whether you are a pastor, missionary, an active lay leader, or simply one of the flock, I challenge you to open your spiritual eyes to see what I'm saying. *You* may even be part of the problem! You may need to take some action to restore blessing.

When will we learn to better discern the enemy's subterfuge and act in authority to subdue it? Typically, openings to enemy infiltration trace to unexposed or unresolved "sin in the camp," among either laity or leadership. This results in a departure of the Lord's favor and a cloud of oppression. As accuser and adversary, the devil takes every advantage of the body's disobedience to God's moral law and works to aggravate unresolved sin. The body of Jesus Christ must seek to maintain both moral purity and unity of the Spirit in order to fully appropriate the Lord's protection from the evil one's accusations.

Let's be reasonable and realistic. Such sins as deceit, malicious anger, bitterness, slander, and the spreading of strife are destructive enough merely on the human level. In church life or in Christian service, all of us have at one time or another been the object of someone's unjustified criticism. On top of the hurt and anger which can consume our time and energy, we always face the temptation to pour out the pain, to share a bitter word about the offender.

We don't need to blame the devil for our flirtation with sensuality or outright involvement in immorality. Sufficient roots of sin remain below the surface of our lives to cause corruption. The sin of unbelief—a refusal to take God's word by faith—is cause enough for deadness and confusion in our corporate life.

Over the years I have met with numerous pastors and leaders of para-church endeavors who suspect satanic oppression at work in their particular group. While this may well be so, I have concluded that we give the devil all he needs with which to work. We provide the entry points when we dilly-dally in dealing with sin issues. We shouldn't be surprised to find ourselves subject to his insidious influence. Yet we often seem blissfully unaware of Satan's schemes to infiltrate the corporate life of our churches.

Demonic entities of strife, sensuality, bitterness, and discouragement actively seek to take advantage of unresolved carnality. James hit that nail squarely on the head: "But if you harbor bitter envy and selfish ambition in your hearts, do not boast about it or deny the truth. Such "wisdom" does not come down from heaven, but is earthly, unspiritual, of the devil. For where you have envy and selfish ambition, there you find disorder and every evil practice" (Jas 3:14-16).

CONSIDERATIONS FOR DISCERNMENT

A number of difficulties can contribute to a loss of God's glory in our church life. Godly leadership is essential. Staff and lay leaders along with the entire congregation must seek the

Lord's voice and direction. The group needs to develop an achievable and relevant vision toward which the whole church can be motivated. Everyone must experience vital worship and praise.

In short, it is too easy to simply pin our corporate problems on the devil. Let's be wise in our analysis of what really ails us. Often a church or organization simply needs a bold change of leadership or a clearer definition of direction. Or, even more importantly, individual members of the church may need to repent of their apathy and compromise with culture and return to seeking the Lord as their first love.

In short, it is too easy to simply pin our corporate problems on the devil. Let's be wise in our analysis of what really ails us.

We can, however, look for some observable signs of "spiritual subterfuge" that may indicate enemy oppression. These signs are based on my personal observations, emerging from many years of consultaton and prayer with pastors and mission leaders. Typically, *sin can be found in the history of the group,* usually at the leadership level. Most often this may involve sexual immorality, prideful ambition, covetousness, or anger. The temptation always surfaces to sweep the problem aside or deal only with its symptoms. Yet until the sin has been dealt with, the overall life of the fellowship will suffer a deadening effect.

Often a breach of trust carries with it a diminished expression of supernatural love. If leadership trust has been violated in the past, the sheep will tend to suspect the integrity of the current shepherd. People will often feel isolated, guarded, self-protective. A tentativeness in commitment may pervade relationships.

Another common sign is *a cloud of confusion in church affairs,* extreme difficulty in getting God's mind and direction for the church. We can expect this if we understand that God has backed away. He will not tolerate unconfessed sin. Real vision deteriorates into divisive individual opinions about what the community should be doing. In this situation, Satan finds additional entry points.

A *distinct deadness and non-responsiveness in worship services* is another major indicator of spiritual oppression. Certainly every church experiences an occasional "flat" worship time when the congregation seems to labor under a corporate lethargy. That happens. There are times when the natural body gets tired. The same can be true of a spiritual corporate body. On other occasions the worship leader or leadership team may be out of step with the Holy Spirit and unwittingly contribute to the deadness. This is normal.

What I am talking about is a demonic heaviness that crushes and quells the worship. Supernatural opposition may be at work to suppress the kind of praise that pleases God and draws forth his presence. Once the people of God come alive to the explosive power of praise, the devil loses his grip.

In any group under attack I also quite commonly find *a person or persons who inject a dominating spirit into the life of the church or organization.* This can take the form of bitterness, strife, control, or rebellion against authority. Whether demonically empowered or not, certain members can wear down the pastor through outright criticism or backstabbing and spreading of gossip.

Such "problem people" can also appear in the guise of righteousness, well-meaning workers who are very involved in service. These members, however, often serve their own agenda rather than the things of God. And when confronted, such individuals are masters of making *you* feel like *you* are the problem! "How dare you confront *me!*"

When a person in a position of power is not broken and submitted to the Lord's will, he or she may become an instrument of influence for demonic powers. The pastoral pathway often becomes slippery. Those in leadership may experience far more than normal discouragement. This kind of battle wears down many pastors and drives them out of the ministry. Such losses can be minimized by better understanding the spiritual warfare dimension of church life.

The gifts of discernment (seeing as God sees) and prophecy

(speaking an utterance prompted by the Holy Spirit) are essential to detect and confront these kinds of influences. Those in leadership should listen to warnings from members of the body who have proven abilities of discernment. Confronting and dealing with "problem people" should only be done after much prayer, and never alone. Decisive, Spirit-guided authority is required to root out those who control others in the wrong ways. Do be sure your own attitude is right before dealing with the confusing mixture of human sin and demonic influence.

DEALING WITH CORPORATE OPPRESSION

You may be thinking, "He's describing my church!" I'm not suggesting that spiritual warfare is any new panacea to resolve church problems. Neither should you sit at the other extreme and ignore these issues. Always remember that God takes sin and its effects far more seriously than we do. If the Lord leads you to suspect something like this might be going on in your fellowship, I offer the following method to clear up sin and remove the oppression.

Many church groups who have followed this procedure, or some modified form of it, have experienced some rather dramatic results. But please, let's be sure to steer clear of another form of legalism. I believe the New Testament church rests under a "grace covering." In any given church, there will be people who are involved in secret sin and compromise. If we had to clean it all up to be free from Satan's devices, every fellowship would be a continual, hopeless mess. I would advise focusing on keeping the committed core members accountable.

Ask relevant, discerning questions. Oppressive strongholds take root for a reason. Do some honest analysis of possible entry points. Acknowledge the possibility that someone may have given ground to the enemy at some point in the past. Talk to your "oldtimers." Ask if they are aware of any unresolved issues like conflicts, offenses, immorality, or bitterness.

Also pursue any current problems. Is your group being disobedient in any way to God's counsel? Are any people grieving the Holy Spirit, causing God to distance himself? Is anyone in a leadership position clinging to control and causing strife? Take careful note of the information you uncover.

Deal wisely with any current sin. If you uncover anything displeasing to God in the current situation, pray and seek direction to deal with it. Scriptural guidelines will help to point you in the right direction (Mt 18:18-20; Gal 6:1; 1 Tm 5:19-20). Even so, the application and follow-through can often be difficult. Confronting and cleaning up sin is a messy business.

Today's environment of threatened lawsuits from disgruntled church members can make this road not only difficult but fearsome. Do your best to gently but decisively bring any parties involved to sincere repentance and reconciliation. In most cases, if those involved are receptive to correction and cooperate with the process, the issues are best dealt with privately. If repentance is resisted, some degree of public disclosure of the matter will need to be pursued.

What to do with past sin. I believe five specific steps can help to resolve sins of the "spiritual forefathers."

1. Confess the sins of the past. Call together your core leaders and explain fully the details that you have uncovered. This process should not involve the whole fellowship since you likely have many newcomers who know nothing about the past. Challenge your leaders beforehand to read and pray through Leviticus 26, Nehemiah 9, and Daniel 9, which speak of offering confession to God on behalf of the sins of "the forefathers." Such a process is essential for full restoration of the health of the body.

In a season of corporate, unhurried prayer, confess the offenses and ask God to restore his favor and the joy of his presence. Believe that he will break and remove the power of any strongholds that may have become entrenched in the fellowship. Leaders must be personally sincere and precise in identifying past offenses, otherwise this will all be a religious, pious exercise.

In one church, the elders were deeply convicted of spiritual pride and self-sufficiency. They took an entire morning service to kneel on the platform, confess their sins and those of the church, and plead with God for mercy. The power of the heart-felt repentance moved the congregation deeply. The leadership team should also be prepared to formally consecrate themselves afresh to the Lord's service.

2. Explain to the church or organization what has happened. Select an appropriate time to explain to the wider fellowship the essence of what the leadership has done—sort of like a "fireside, family chat." You don't need to hang out all the dirty laundry, unless the Lord leads you to be specific. Be general; be positive. If you are facing a current sin situation in which the offender is unrepentant, follow the Matthew 18 procedure for church discipline.

The important thing is that you let the people know that the leadership has taken sin very seriously and has already gone before the Lord to confess it and seek his mercy. Most people will be satisfied with this. If some still have questions, answer them privately. Some will likely have been more seriously affected by the "time in the wilderness" and will require additional personal care.

3. Call the fellowship to fresh vision and consecration. This can be an enormously positive time. Build an altar of remembrance. Put the past behind as the people make a sincere consecration of themselves to the Lord's purposes. This will help to restore confidence in the godliness of the leadership. Challenge those who are accustomed to fasting to offer this as a sacrifice to the Lord. I recommend focusing on Solomon's prayer of dedication for the new temple as recorded in 2 Chronicles 6 and 7.

4. Cleanse the property of any demonic presence. Paul admonished the Ephesian church to "have nothing to do with the fruitless deeds of darkness, but rather expose them" (Eph. 5:11). Bringing darkness into the light destroys its power. Expose the enemy's footholds and strongholds. With your mature leaders, walk through your facility and claim each room for the Lord's glory. In prayer, apply the name and the blood of Jesus to remove the power of any enemy influence. Apply these prayers to specific rooms where offenses were known to have occurred.

Ask God to break the power of any curses or demonic assaults that came against you during this time. Invite the Holy Spirit to fill and occupy your facility and to drive out anything unclean or evil. I've talked to many pastors and laymen who have gone through this procedure. Some have felt awkward, even silly marching about the facility praying in such an unfamiliar way. But everyone has reported the blessing of having done it. God will honor your obedience.

Such an exercise opens us to further instruction, honors the Lord, and many times produces measurable results. I led this kind of an effort for a major para-church group for an entire day. Their property had been penetrated by New Age and demonic influences and they had been fighting a noticeable oppression. Some of the more conservative types were rather iffy on how to proceed, but God poured his presence out in a mighty way and sealed this group's spiritual borders.

When a church or Christian fellowship remains healthy
and overflowing with the fullness of Christ,
unsaved persons will be drawn to you like moths to a lightbulb.

---

5. Institute ongoing, regular prayer. After regaining lost ground, continue to seek the Lord for vision and direction. Many churches now have either a Saturday night or Sunday morning prayer group that petitions God to anoint the services, the message, the morning musicians, and the worship. Many like to pray through the worship auditorium, at the pulpit and over the seats, inviting God to work his will in the hearts of the people.

Challenge this praying core to believe God will bring revival to the churches of your city. Ask God to pour out a spirit of conviction of sin among the lost. Pray for specific groupings of people in your area as well as names of individuals. Remember: when a church or Christian fellowship remains healthy and overflowing with the fullness of Christ, unsaved persons will be drawn to you like moths to a lightbulb.

A CASE HISTORY

I recently conducted a meeting in a church in a large metropolitan area, by invitation of the pastor. He had come alive to teaching on spiritual warfare and wanted his people to get "the full shot." In the Saturday morning session, I presented the contents of this chapter. I had no idea where my sharing would lead.

The pastor had already scheduled a Saturday evening session with the leadership team, staff, deacons, teachers, home Bible study leaders, youth workers, etc. Around sixty people came out for a fireside chat. I was already generally aware that the church had labored through a hard history, with four pastors in six years.

When I asked for any response to my morning teaching, the problems began surfacing. Two pastors had left the church under a cloud of misunderstanding, angry and embittered. The leadership had remained sharply divided concerning the release of one of them. Another pastor had struggled so deeply with depression that he ended up drowning himself in a nearby river. I was told that he even used to stand in the baptistry and contemplate suicide.

At this point, an older woman added a sobering note: "Over the years, I've heard people in this city say, 'We know about *that* church… it has a curse on it!'" Then another woman began to cry. She felt that the church was still carrying a "spirit of grief or heaviness" as a result of that pastor's suicide. Corporately, the church had never resolved this painful issue. Events like this are often too traumatic and perplexing to process at the time.

For another hour or so, others shared names of men and women who had been hurt or offended in past years. Commitments were made openly to talk to some of these people in order to seek forgiveness and restitution. The evening closed with the whole group moving spontaneously to their knees in sincere repentance for the past and commitment to righteousness in the future. God was powerfully at work to restore favor and blessing to his people.

The morning services the next day felt like someone had opened a window. I preached a message, then the pastor took the end of the service. His initiative demonstrates the necessity of godly, courageous leadership and the commitment to do the right thing. With a careful balance of discretion and truthfulness, the pastor reported to the congregation the essence of what had happened the night before. He reaffirmed his personal commitment to continue to lead the church and asked for continued prayer. As he spoke, I perceived in my own spirit the Lord's pleasure.

Months after the above incident, I keep getting reports that this fellowship has "turned a spiritual corner" and that the body is healthy and growing. I pray that others who read this account and implement this procedure will find similar refreshment in the fellowship of the redeemed. This I know: The Lord of the church stands ready to act on our behalf if we will take appropriate steps to honor him.

We owe our Bridegroom an honest evaluation of our attitudes and behaviors, past and present. We should be committed to living a life worthy of his name. The renewal movement currently underway offers great hope that the bride of Christ will exhibit a purity and supernatural presence in the eyes of a world searching for answers that make sense to life's ultimate questions.

Before you talk about pursuing a vision for evangelism in your community, you should seal the corporate cracks and secure the perimeter. Then, and only then, will you inhabit a position of "holiness in the Lord" to stand against the schemes of the evil one that keep people from coming into the kingdom of God.

7

Understanding Strategic Warfare

I T WAS EASTER MORNING, 1985. I won't soon forget it. Two vans and a passenger car slowly cut through the fog of a damp Oregon morning. The riders seemed subdued, half asleep and struggling with secret doubts about the assignment. I popped in the praise tape I had prepared to stir the hearts of my motley spiritual marines. "Holy, holy, holy, Lord God Almighty, early in the morning our song shall rise to thee!"

Fourteen brothers and sisters from seven different churches had responded to my call for a pre-dawn assault on Mary's Peak, the highest mountain in the coastal range, a spiritual stronghold in our area. The original Indian name for this coastal mountain was *"Timanwi,"* which means "place of spirit power" or "place where the spirits dwell." Mary's Peak had recently become a known hang-out for occult ritualists and local witches.

We agreed it was time to reclaim the ground, proclaim Jesus as King of the mid-Willamette Valley, and weaken the grip of darkness over the land. Burdened for our city, our valley, for the state of Oregon, we felt like pioneers pressing into enemy territory. The others were following me, presuming that I knew what I was doing. The only thing I knew for sure was that I was following Jesus.

No glorious sunrise heralded the dawn on this mountain shrouded in fog. As we hiked toward the peak, a bone-chilling rain settled in. I could feel my Gideon's band lagging and dragging with doubt. *Is this really going to accomplish anything? This is kind of nuts!* Frankly, I felt a bit nuts myself! Sometimes obeying the Lord looks and feels a bit foolish from the human perspective. I remember thinking, *this must be what they felt like hiking around Jericho.*

When we reached the top, I drew our focus to two victorious verses from the Psalms: "Every morning I will put to silence all the wicked in the land" (Ps 101:8); "The scepter of the wicked will not remain over the land allotted to the righteous" (Ps 125:3). I had prepared an instruction sheet to guide our prayer effort.

Together we read aloud the following statement of purpose: "In obedience to the Lord, we purpose to make a stand both verbal and visible to expose, resist, and weaken the forces of darkness at work in the Willamette Valley. We are called to courageous faith in claiming this territory for the glory of God and in interceding for his servants and for the spread of the truth of the gospel."

Suddenly it didn't seem to matter that we were standing in forty-two miserable, wet degrees. A fresh faith arose in our hearts to diminish the doubts. The presence of Jesus, our Commander-in-Chief, sealed our purpose. In unity of heart, in agreement in his name, and with unwavering faith, we stood in the soaking rain singing praises to our resurrected King.

For the next ninety minutes, the Spirit of God sovereignly prompted prayers of blessing on the leaders and churches of the Willamette Valley. We petitioned the Lord to pierce and weaken the satanic darkness in our area. Applying the blood of Christ, we revoked the effects of rituals and curses spoken from Mary's Peak. What had at first seemed wild and weird quickly turned into an achievement of victorious obedience. We finished our assignment that day with a warm sense of God's pleasure.

Though it may have seemed insignificant and unproductive at the time, our little SWAT team (Spiritual Warfare Action Team) poured out prayers of investment that were guaranteed an eventual return.

Did this prayer effort have anything to do with the current spiritual awakening occurring among the pastors and churches of our valley? I believe it did. Though it may have seemed insignificant and unproductive at the time, our little SWAT team (Spiritual Warfare Action Team) poured out prayers of investment that were guaranteed an eventual return. Guaranteed because we had been obedient to the voice of God and because our petitions blended with those of other intercessors praying for the valley. And because, even in our human weakness, we had acted in faith.

WARNING: HANDLE WITH PRAYER

Up to this point we've been examining strongholds that relate to ourselves, other unsaved persons, and the church. I want you to look now at a wider perspective. Bigger battles roar around us, with even higher stakes. The Bible warns us of satanic powers that exert influence over cities, counties, regions, even whole nations.

Does the Word of God offer any direction about how to deal with the powers of darkness at this level? We know that righteous Old Testament kings sent out the people to tear down the "high places" of paganism. We aren't told *how* it was done, but we know *that* it was done. Can we apply these kinds of examples to modern spiritual warfare?

Let's understand right up front that this level of warfare is not for everyone. It is for men and women called and equipped by God to seek his strategy in standing against darkness. You may be a homemaker, a college student, a business executive, or a retiree. God may be raising you up to be a spiritual warrior. If so, make sure your leading is clear. Check your motives and be committed to cleaning up your own backyard first.

A word to the wise: don't be overly eager to sign up for the kingdom special forces unit. Intercessory warfare is no picnic. When you press against satanic strongholds, the devil pushes back. Strategic warfare initiated outside the will of God opens doors for oppression, infirmity, family problems, even the loss of your role of service or ministry. God calls all of us to resist the evil one to some degree. Any SWAT team is doomed to failure without support personnel, a communications team, supply reinforcements, and transportation specialists. We can find no cause for personal glory in this joint effort. In what way might the Lord want you to enter into this bigger battle?

I'm convinced God is raising such an army today, but we must be careful to wage the war with divine wisdom and weapons. This level of warfare involves not so much confrontation with powers of darkness as it does intercession. We must not take the resolution of evil into our own hands, but rather move God's hands through prayer and obedience.

The Lord appointed Jeremiah "to uproot and tear down, to destroy and overthrow, to build and to plant" (Jer 1:10). Four negatives and two positives. *Evil must be supplanted by the Word of the Lord and righteousness implanted. Intercession alone can accomplish such a task.*

Can we boldly expect to rid our cities of demonic darkness with a "go get 'em" magical prayer against principalities? We dare not. Such an approach would be both dangerous and unbiblical. I am not advocating a subtle form of "Christian magic." As we seek to obey God's call to subdue the influence of evil and to turn men, women, and children to righteousness, we must avoid any hint of grandstanding or bandwagoning.

You may think I'm sending mixed signals. "On the one hand,

do this kind of praying. On the other hand, don't touch it." Strategic warfare certainly needs to be handled with care. God alone must be our mentor. I simply encourage you to learn his ways and let him do through you whatever he chooses.

God graciously guides us through our failures. I've made a lot of mistakes and many readjustments over the years. I've learned the importance of remaining focused on what *God* is doing rather than speculating about what *Satan* seems to be doing. I'm convinced we are to be about praying to God to move with power among his people rather than shouting the devil out of our cities.

I advocate a fourfold focus to keep the practice of strategic intercession balanced and biblical. We must pray for the *renewal* of God's presence and fullness in the church, the *redemption* of the lost, *resistance* against the enemy's schemes, and moral *reformation* of our culture. We have thus far concentrated on church renewal and personal redemption. With this kingdom agenda clearly in mind, let's explore this special call to behind-the-enemy-lines "resistance" in greater detail.

WHAT DO THE SCRIPTURES SAY?

Most of you will have no difficulty believing that evil spirits harass and oppress people. But do particular territorial spirits— "celestial strongmen" of sorts—work in certain cities, areas, or countries? If so, how do they manifest themselves? How would we know one if we met one? These are big questions, scary questions. I have seen many a zealous believer going off half-cocked on a holy crusade to poke holes in the gates of hell because it seemed like the right thing to do. But is this a right use of authority? Is it *God's way* of overcoming evil?

Let's examine the evidence in the Scriptures. The Old Testament describes particular places preferred for pagan worship practices, namely on mountaintops and under certain trees (Dt 12:2). In the midst of a series of battles with the Arameans, a man of God came to the king of Israel with these words: "'Because the Arameans think the Lord is a god of the hills and not a god of the valleys, I will deliver this vast army into your hands'" (1 Kgs 20:28). Because they believed in territorial spirits, the pagans understood Israel's God as holding territorial strength. Now just because pagans believed it doesn't make it so, but we do see reflected here the common worldview of the day.

After the king of Assyria had captured Samaria, he started to resettle the area with his people. Because they did not worship the God of Israel, the following report came back to the king: "The people you deported and resettled in the towns of Samaria do not know what the god of that country requires. He has sent lions among them, which are killing them off, because the people do not know what he requires" (2 Kgs 17:26).

We are then told that each nationality set up its own gods, shrines, and high places in their individual towns (v. 29). We see in this story more evidence of territorial spirits, particularized places of power. Who were these "gods"? They were fallen, satanic spirits who sought the adulation and sacrifices of unenlightened peoples.

The Apostle Paul casts the clearest light on this topic by warning us that we wrestle against many kinds and classes of dark forces. We just cannot know for certain the identification and ranking of these "principalities, powers, thrones, spiritual forces of wickedness" (Eph 6:12). (I have already shared my understanding of his insights in chapter two of my first book, *The Believer's Guide to Spiritual Warfare*.) Paul's writings do indicate, however, that such fallen powers connect with earthly governments and institutions.

I believe we can state a general principle here: *demons are drawn to people and places where they are invited.* There are places and spaces of dark power. Why did Paul have so much trouble in Ephesus? Because it was the very center of the cult of Artemis, the "Queen of Heaven," the pagan fertility goddess.

When the city clerk tried to quiet a riot stirred by Paul's preaching, note what he said: "'Men of Ephesus, doesn't all the world know that the city of Ephesus is the guardian of the temple of the great Artemis and of her image, which fell from heaven?'" (Acts 19:35). An image that "fell from heaven"! A fallen deity finding residence on earth. Also take note of Jesus' letter to the church at Pergamum, "where Satan has his throne" (Rv 2:13). Pergamum was a place of unusual occult power.

I believe we can state a general principle here: demons are drawn to people and places where they are invited. There are places and spaces of dark power.

While the Bible does not explicitly define the existence of territorial spirits, I am convinced such references indicate the existence of demons that are given open doors of control in certain geographical places. George Otis, missions researcher and pioneer of "spiritual mapping," sheds further light on this question: "While God is the rightful head of human *families* (ethnos—tribes and people groups), Satan is in general control over human *systems* (kosmos—kingdoms and structures). Whereas God's authority is derived through *fatherhood*, Satan's rule, in the latter instance, is achieved through the *volition of men.*"[1] Such ruling demonic spirits seek to maintain influence in a place until they are exposed, weakened, and potentially expelled by the presence of the kingdom of Christ. God and his angels alone can know the impact in the heavenlies of our obedience on earth.

WHAT DOES EXPERIENCE TELL US?

Have you ever taken a vacation and found yourself feeling spiritually uncomfortable in a particular place? I have felt such an uneasiness on certain Indian reservations in the southwestern United States, perhaps because of the history of animism connected to Native American religion. Hindu shrines in India or Buddhist temples in Taiwan and Thailand often stir the same discomfort. Just last year my son Joshua and I noticed this as we walked through some of the major Shinto temples in Japan.

I believe many of us have had experiences in such places where we feel we have just entered a foreign spiritual territory. How would you know? You may feel uncomfortable, like you're intruding. You might be gripped with an unexplained fear or wrestle with doubts about your faith. You might notice a headache or a loss of energy. Moms traveling with their children have reported an intense protection instinct—a strong desire to get their kids away from a certain place. You might even sense a heaviness or uncleanness about a specific city, shrine, or park.

These are often "signals" of the ruling presence of foreign, fallen spirits in a particular location. Picture a malicious spiritual governor, watching for anyone who would intrude on his or her territory. The reigning deity would make you feel uncomfortable, unwanted. I am not sharing this out of speculation. I think many of us have had such experiences. We need not feel threatened or paranoid, but rather wise and discerning.

Often when we vacation in the Oregon Cascades, we drive through one of my least favorite towns. Years ago I began to notice that I kind of "got the creeps" and couldn't get through there fast enough! The place felt somehow "unclean." I have since learned that this town has had the highest per capita occurrence of domestic sexual abuse of any place in the nation. Spirits of lust and violence were rampant in that town! Why? Because of many people's volitional indulgence in particular sins.

The Pacific Northwest is known these days as a favorite habitation for New Age seekers. When I visit certain cities in this area, I can perceive (I avoid the word "feel," because it's not emotion) the presence of evil spirits. Ministering in a particular midwestern city has always been very challenging for me. My kingdom endeavors there always seem to be obstructed or "uphillish." A major center for organized satanism and other forms of witchcraft, that city is also home to religious traditionalism, a form of "churchianity" devoid of the power of the Spirit of God. The lack of spiritual vitality gives added place and power to the darkness.

Am I connecting with your experience in any way? As you reflect on past trips and experiences, is the Lord giving you any added discernment? I believe personal spirit-beings wield power over peoples and places, but their influence is often masked by institutions such as governments, religious organizations, the media, the movie industry, and underground crime. Often you can't point a finger and say, "Look at that demon!" But you can certainly say, "Look at the availability of violence and pornography. That's demonic!"

Since we wrestle against *invisible* forces of wickedness, we see and sense the *effect* more clearly than we can perceive the *cause*. I believe more of us must come to understand this. Then we can begin to mobilize our efforts appropriately in prayer to overcome evil—God's way.

THE HEART OF THE MATTER: LOVE IN ACTION

Having considered this question of strategic warfare for some years now, let me define more precisely what I mean. *Strategic spiritual warfare is the endeavor of an individual or group of mature believers to move out in the authority of the Word of God, anointed by the Spirit of God, to expose and overthrow the kingdom of darkness, and to significantly advance the kingdom of light.* To be successful, we need to wait for the revelation of the Lord's purposes, persist in intercessory prayer, and identify with the heart of God for renewal in the church, redemption of the lost, and the reformation of society.

The primary activity envisioned in strategic warfare is *intercession* before the throne of God, not *interaction* with fallen principalities. We *are not* called to wield laser beams of biblical authority to destroy heavenly strongholds. We *are* called to destroy in the lives of people (Christian and non-Christian) "strongholds... arguments and every pretension that sets itself up against the knowledge of God" (2 Cor 10:4, 5). We are called to faithfully reflect the glory of Jesus Christ through our obedience to his commands.

This important difference in approach produces a profoundly different result. Strategic spiritual warfare means pursuing the presence of Christ and aligning ourselves with his purposes. We are not assigned to zealously launch spiritual "surface-to-air missiles" into the heavenlies, or lob gospel-grenades into presumed enemy bunkers. If we get caught up in this kind of "commando mentality," we run the risk of running ahead of the Lord in fleshly zeal. Strategic warfare must originate from a dependent brokenness, must be directed by the Holy Spirit, and must be initiated at the opportune time.

Strategic warfare must originate from a dependent brokenness, must be directed by the Holy Spirit, and must be initiated at the opportune time.

Tactical models. Various models of strategic prayer are popping up in many places. Let me categorize these simply as "confrontive," "moderate," and "conservative." There are some today who lead city-wide efforts to mobilize the praise and prayer of local saints to break the ruling powers of darkness over that place. The approach is highly confrontive. Presumably, the goal is to weaken and drive territorial spirits out of a city. While this approach sounds appealing in its immediacy, its lack of biblical support leaves it deficient and potentially dangerous. I cannot endorse this particular approach to spiritual warfare. I can find no biblical precedent for trying to stage such a short-term "knock-out punch." I seriously question the appropriateness of some of the more public methods. My own experience suggests the ineffectiveness of trying to drive evil spirits from heavenly strongholds before the hearts of the residents are broken over the sin that gives place to the strongholds to begin with. We run the risk of stirring up the wrath of demonic beings and incurring a counterattack we're not prepared to handle. The proliferation of self-styled spiritual commandos makes me nervous.

Other moderate, balanced approaches better fit the biblical parameters because they present prayer, reconciliation of relationships, and evangelism as key ingredients of a warfare strategy. I think of John Dawson of Youth With a Mission (author of *Taking Our Cities for God*) and Francis Frangipane (author of *The Three Battlegrounds* and *The House of the Lord*). Dick Eastman (author of *Love on its Knees*) has practiced this kind of prayer for years with profound results.

Francis Frangipane serves as a pastor-at-large of a fellowship in Cedar Rapids, Iowa, that continues to develop a powerful model of strategic, city-wide intercession. His understanding of "binding and loosing" captures the essence of this moderate approach to spiritual warfare:

> Notice that Jesus gave the same instruction for two seemingly different situations. The context of Matthew 16:18-19 deals with the devil, while the focus of Matthew 18:15-18 is sin. These realms are interconnected. The sinfulness of mankind, his evil thoughts, words and actions, is the very shelter of the devil over our cities! Since this is true, then righteousness in the church proportionately displaces the devil in the spirit realm, offering Satan no hiding place. He may tempt, but he cannot abide. Indeed, when the church truly draws near to God, the devil flees.[2]

Proponents of the moderate approach strongly emphasize unity of local leadership, the centrality of prayer, and the priority of dealing with strongholds within the church as preconditions for an aggressive posture against strongholds outside of the church.

The *conservative* approach to strategic praying is modeled by

David Bryant, evangelical leader and founder of the Concerts of Prayer movement. (A second model for conservative city-reaching warfare is Northwest Renewal Ministries, in Portland, Oregon. I will share a specific example in chapter nine describing its emphasis.) Bryant recognizes the role of resisting satanic forces in prayer as a dimension of proclaiming victory in Christ. But he is also quick to caution that a confrontive approach with weak biblical precedent holds potential for getting us diverted from the primary object of our prayer. Controversy sparked by the confrontive models can also cause divisiveness in the body.

At a meeting of the Spiritual Warfare Network in Pasadena, Bryant described a recent Concert of Prayer gathering in a midwestern city where black and white pastors stood together on the platform and confessed racial prejudice and sins of mistrust for one another. Many of them embraced and publicly modeled the victory of Jesus' love in overcoming such barriers. "That," said Bryant, "*speaks* destruction to the powers of darkness." He is right. This surely is a mode of spiritual warfare.

A strategy for overcoming evil must be based on the power released in and through a church broken and obedient to her Lord.

We are called to live the mystery of the gospel and manifest the glory of the Lord through our obedience in loving one another and walking in integrity. The primary battle is thus not "out there," but in submitting to Christ fully as Lord in our own hearts. Paul's burden for the church at Ephesus was that they, as a body, "be filled to the measure of all the fullness of God" (Eph 3:19). When the Holy Spirit fills, he automatically displaces the power of sin and Satan. The regular practice of prayer and worship rooted in mutual love opens the door to such fullness.

A strategy for overcoming evil must be based on the power

released in and through a church broken and obedient to her Lord. The picture in the book of Ephesians is of a church endowed with the experience of Jesus' loving presence. They were characterized by an ongoing unity in the Spirit, healthy relationships, and a posture of responsible warfare against the powers of darkness. In such a climate, the initiative for strategic advance remains in the hands of God. Our responsibility is to read those signals in prayer and act in timely ways. When Jesus reigns supreme in our individual hearts and churches, geographical strongholds will be weakened.

Freed from apathy and self-sufficiency, a renewed church will care about the needs of the people it is called to serve. It will take bold steps of obedience which will automatically expose and weaken darkness. Ministry to the poor, counseling for the abused, crisis pregnancy help for unwed mothers, involvement in racial reconciliation—these are only a few of the means of doing justice that validate the presence and relevance of the kingdom.

"Live as children of light... have nothing to do with the fruitless deeds of darkness, but rather expose them" (Eph 5:8-11). The tangible incarnation of Jesus' love does more to expose and expel evil from our cities than all of our words, programs, and strategic plans combined. Love in action is the heart of the matter.

THE KEY TO KINGDOM ADVANCEMENT

If love in action is the heart of the matter, then what is the key which unlocks this love? *Remaining under divine authority is the key to kingdom advancement.* If you are humbly walking with Jesus and stripped of self-will, the Master will give you his own heart and lead you in claiming captives for Christ. He will prompt you not only to recognize spiritual battles but he will also empower you to emerge victorious.

Some years back I organized a prayer meeting for local church members on Halloween night, one of the unholy days for witches and cult satanists. We were scheduled to pray in one church from 6:30 to 8:00 and then across town in another church from 8:30 to 10:00. The saints showed up to pray. Our time was pleasing to the Lord and productive, but I didn't particularly sense any great power in either location.

What I didn't expect was the anointing that came on me as I drove from one meeting to the other. Passing the fraternity houses near the university, I suddenly felt God's heart for those who were separated from him. As I drove, I poured out intense prayers, proclaiming the pre-eminence of Christ over our city and penetrating strongholds of darkness with the power of praise. "The reason the Son of God appeared was to destroy the devil's work" (1 Jn 3:8). I was simply on assignment, acting in my Lord's authority.

At specific times and in particular places, God calls seasoned believers, sensitive to the stirrings of the Spirit, to step into the battle. On these occasions the wrestlings of the heavenlies converge in our own hearts and compel us to act in an authority beyond ourselves. Here is a simple way in which I describe the human progression of this divinely ordained compulsion:

1. *Abiding:* We cultivate a relationship with God.
2. *Appropriation:* We receive divine authority.
3. *Action:* We step out by faith.
4. *Anointing:* Our efforts are empowered by God.
5. *Advancement:* We see the Lord's kingdom gain ground.

Abiding, remaining in God's presence through obedience to his Word, poises us in readiness and leads to an *appropriation of divine authority.* God then has the option of drawing us into action. This is where we wrestle: *Lord is this you? Am I really supposed to pray, or share a word, or engage that person in dialogue?*

Action involves stepping out of our comfort zones. If we have the courage to move on what we believe to be divinely inspired impulses, we step into the *anointing*. If the initiative truly comes from God, we experience a divine strength that lifts us out of human weakness. If it's not, our effort will be futile. If God is in the assignment, the way is clear—not always easy—clear!

What begins as an impression or gentle impulse in our minds will connect with real life events. God graciously confirms his instructions. And in some measure, whether in the planting of seeds of truth, the salvation of a person, a timely prayer for a Christian leader, or the weakening of a local stronghold, the Lord's kingdom moves ahead. This *advancement* of the kingdom brings glory to God.

As you grow in the depth of your own personal prayer life, you will more and more clearly perceive God's burdens. Ask the Lord for assignments. You'll never be the same. Every day becomes an adventure. It's like walking through life with one ear open to human reality, while the other ear is wired to receive transmissions from the command post of heaven.

Let love always be your aim as you put divine authority into action. In commenting on the qualifications for doing strategic warfare, Frangipane offers this critical word of advice: "Authority is muscle in the arm of love. The more one loves, the more authority is granted to him.... However, no man should ever engage in confrontational warfare who does not love what he has been called to protect. If you do not love your city, do not pray against the ruling forces of darkness."[3]

Will you hear and heed this word? If you move out ahead of the Lord in your *own* power, expect counterattack. I have seen people suffer from depression, tension in marital or family relationships, extreme confusion, and health problems. The satanic power "out there" will push back. If we move at God's command and remain accountable and accessible to others, he will surely shield us from the powers of darkness and bring success to our efforts.

DISCERNING AND DEALING WITH STRONGHOLDS

Is it possible to accurately discern particular strongholds? Following are some steps we can take to clearly identify enemy outposts.

How can we know? The discernment of strongholds is a slippery business. I've had so many people tell me that a certain strongman rules over a city or place. How can we *know* this? A Christian receives knowledge from three sources: 1) the special revelation of Scripture (2 Tm 3:16-17); 2) the inspiration of the Holy Spirit (Jn 16:13; 1 Cor 2:9-16); and 3) the general revelation of creation.

When involved in strategic warfare, you would be wise to look at particular supernatural forces revealed in the Bible. Instead of being quick to grab or guess at the identity of a fallen power, look first to the Word. For example, a cursory look reveals the following major "spirits" of darkness: Dagon (Jgs 16:23), Molech (Lv 20:2), the Queen of Heaven (Jer 44:17), Ashteroth (1 Kgs 11:33), Artemis (Acts 19:24-35), Zeus (Acts 14:11), Hermes (Acts 14:11), the "Princes" (Daniel 10), and Apollyon (Rv 9:11).

Biblically, we understand that these demonic beings may require blood sacrifice, sexual indulgence, or direct worship. The same angelic beings that tempted Israel tempt us today and even use the same tactics. There is nothing new under the sun. These demons may merely change their names and create a new "front of operation" suitable to modern sophistication. And I do not believe that learning the name of a ruling Spirit is necessary to overcome its influence. Seeking to know names is a speculative and slippery matter.

We shouldn't have to guess at such matters with human reason. We can do a thorough biblical survey of the deceptive, fallen powers and then superimpose that survey over the current situation. I have heard some of the most bizarre names given for ruling spirits. Who knows if they're really "out there"? But we know the fallen gods and goddesses of the Bible are really "out there." For example, I believe that "the great prostitute...

Babylon the Great" of Revelation 17 is in fact the most blatant manifestation of occult religion with origins in ancient times. We don't need to grope about trying to detect the principle players of hell.

With the discernment the Holy Spirit gives us, we may follow two approaches in gaining clearer knowledge. Either one, or a combination of both, may help us to better know the nature of a territorial enemy. *Inspirational induction* relies primarily upon the revelatory work of the Spirit, working through his gifts. You move from specific revelation (either Scripture or an impression from the Spirit) outward to the situation.

This process usually involves various spiritual giftings (for example, discerning of spirits, words of knowledge, and prophecy). We enjoy a great advantage but also face a grave danger in this approach. The advantage is clear: if God speaks, the information is reliable and the right application of that truth will produce a positive result.

However, the impression may come from your own mind—perhaps you are an over-zealous warrior in search of a stronghold. Or the impression could even come via a demon—perhaps the enemy creating "rabbit trails." We face the danger of going ahead of God, or without him altogether. We must cultivate a practice of waiting on God in prolonged periods of Scripture meditation, prayer, and fasting. Only then, in my view, will he impart an accurate reading of the spiritual climate of a city or region.

Some of you might feel more at ease with a sort of "sanctified scientific" approach, an *observational deduction* of sorts. With Scripture in hand, we move from observation of general conditions (a high occurrence of domestic violence, cultic activity, demonic manifestations) back to a presumed cause (a certain territorial spirit).

You can sometimes glean this information by observing the type of spiritual bondage suffered by both Christians and non-Christians in a certain place. Interviews with key leaders who have served in a particular environment can also prove helpful.

The drawback of this approach is getting bogged down in observational detail or coming to the wrong reasonable conclusions.

How do we know if *what* we know is accurate? The only test of accuracy is the "wait and see" test (cf. the test of a true prophet in Dt 18:21-22 and 1 Thes 5:19-22, or the wisdom of Gamaliel in Acts 5:33-39). Our military satellites can spot a presumed deployment of a chemical rocket. We cannot *know* for sure what it is until we get our hands on it or until it explodes.

The doing of supernatural business can be just as slippery. If the knowledge upon which we pray and minister has its origins in God, our endeavors will result in measurable fruit. This is true both biblically and historically.

We must ask a question here. How can we know if the negative influence in a given spiritual environment originates primarily from the heavenlies downward or from the corrupt hearts of men outward? Before we plunge into projects designed to weaken "territorial spirits" (we hope to be agents of positive change for the populace) we must consider the possibility that the greater bondage may rest with the wickedness of human hearts.

In short, supernatural deception would have no power were it not for people's vulnerability to it. How can we be so sure that a cultural preoccupation with greed, lust, or violence points unquestionably toward a supernatural entity? Several years ago I saw a map pinpointing the ruling spirits over counties and cities in the San Francisco Bay area. Over San José and the Silicon Valley was listed "SELF." I ask an honest question: is there really such a personal spirit being or is this merely an observation of an element of human fallenness focused in one place? It is not clear to me how to know for sure that such a "strong man" actually exists.

Whether we operate from the inductive or deductive approach, this element of confirmation remains crucial. We must require an affirmative witness from the Spirit of God (such as a word, prophecy, dream), the written Word, or fellow servants known to be sensitive to the voice of God. Such a confirming witness can say to the person on the point of strategic advance, "You are seeing correctly; proceed." Do your best to discern, then trust the Lord to confirm what you see.

My conviction is that we are to become so broken, yielded, and sensitive to the Spirit's movement that we resolve not to move into aggressive prayer unless we are "picked up" by the Lord and put into a place of compelling action.

How do we know when to *do* **something with what we know?** It's hard to speak of discernment apart from considering what we are to *do* with what we know. If you're anything like me, you have a hard time "sitting on" information. If someone is convinced that a certain spirit rules in a region, that knowledge (even if accurate) does not necessitate action.

Here again, the leaping-before-looking danger applies. My conviction is that we are to become so broken, yielded, and sensitive to the Spirit's movement that we resolve not to move into aggressive prayer unless we are "picked up" by the Lord and put into a place of compelling action. Historically, a select few have been sovereignly so moved to engage darkness at this level. But —and this is a major but—God *is* picking up his praying people today and compelling them into strategic intercession.

Timing in strategic praying—being aligned with the will of the Father and flowing with the promptings of the Spirit—is crucial. If a soldier of Christ moves with inaccurate or presumptive discernment, counterattack can be tragic. Even if you have made an accurate spiritual diagnosis, you are still in danger of injecting your own eagerness or resolve into the matter and moving out ahead of God. Your efforts can fall to the ground, unfruitful. If you move out in proper motivation, but with inaccurate information, you may be in no great harm, but you could be considerably misdirected and distracted from more fruitful ministry.

What conclusions can we draw about strategic spiritual warfare? As followers of Jesus, we are called to do what the Master did (Jn 14:12): proclaim reconciliation, make disciples, heal the sick, and cast out demons. We may courageously involve ourselves in deliverance work. We are to expose evil when we discern it (Eph 5:11), yet speak blessing to the evildoer (Mt 5:44; Rom 12:17-21) in hopes of leading that person into the light of Christ.

The church is to stand firm in order to extinguish the fiery darts of evil as they come at us (Eph 6:10-18), being alert to the enemy's schemes (2 Cor 11:3, 14; 1 Pt 5:8). We are given practical instruction on how to "resist the devil" until he flees (Jas 4:6-10). The conditions for such resistance are all centered on strengthening our personal relationship with the Lord.

We are called to live the mystery of love, demonstrating the miraculous unity that is possible only in Christ (Eph 3:1-13). We are exhorted to pray earnestly for those in positions of governmental authority (1 Tm 2:1-2), that the gospel may be lived and promoted. This Spirit-led proclamation of truth through the obedience of the children of light is the normal means of advancing the kingdom.

But should we expect occasional *extraordinary* means of expanding light in the darkness? Yes. This ought not to be a question of *either* daily ministry *or* strategic warfare. Both are valid dimensions of kingdom expansion. The building of the church is ordinary and inclusive. Confronting powers of darkness in biblical authority is extraordinary and occasional, and is carried out by spirit-selected (not elitist) vessels. In the face of the increasing flood of evil in our day, I believe God is strengthening us to recognize our struggle with supernatural evil in order to restrain its influence. I believe God is raising up men and women of faith to lead the body in strategic, focused prayer. The primary focus of this commission will be to penetrate the remaining satanic strongholds in our world in preparation for the coming harvest. Let's turn now to some specific instruction on how, what, and when to pray strategically.

8

Watching over
Our Cities

I have posted watchmen on your walls, O Jerusalem;
they will never be silent day or night. You who call on the LORD,
give yourselves no rest, and give him no rest till he establishes
Jerusalem and makes her the praise of the earth. **Is 62:6**

I WAS VERY FAR FROM HOME that mid-Saturday afternoon, with only about an hour remaining in a prayer and spiritual warfare seminar. As I stood before this group of thirty-three saints learning to be soldiers, I felt the Lord nudge me with the idea of leading some strategic prayer for the city that evening: in Budapest, Hungary. I shared the prompting at the close of my teaching, honestly expecting five to ten people to take me up on it. Every person in the room wanted to participate.

We packed ourselves into several vehicles and headed for a hillside park which overlooks both sides of this beautiful Eastern European city. I knew by now that the prompting was not just a personal whim. These greenhorn soldiers rode in solemn quietness as they prepared to pray for their city.

Reassembled in the park, our group looked out over the two sides of the city, Buda and Pest, separated by the serenely flowing Danube River. We discovered a new bronze statue resting on the hillside. The statue depicted a stately king reaching out to a beautiful bronze maiden, symbolizing the two different sides of the city. That statue spoke volumes about the reunion and harmony we so desired for the body of Christ in this city.

We began to intercede for the church of Budapest. At one point, quite spontaneously, a key leader from a charismatic fellowship moved to the side of the maiden. This man placed his hands behind her and leaned in toward the middle, pushing. The leader of the main evangelical church crossed over to the other side of the statue and placed his hands behind the king, also pushing toward the middle. It was an absolutely holy moment. The pleasure of the Lord's presence poured out upon us as we interceded for the unity and strength of the church in that city and for salvation of those still lost. On that day, in that place, God sovereignly posted our little band on the walls of Budapest.

Do you want to learn more about putting this kind of prayer into practice? Even though you may feel inadequate and uncertain, the Lord is nudging you forward. I know the feeling. You can't just work up this kind of motivation on a human level. Intercession is spiritual work. Having God's heart involves carrying his burdens for the church and for the lost. I want to share as simply as possible some direction first on *how to pray* strategically, then more precisely *what to pray*, and last, *what forms such praying might take.*

BEARING THE LORD'S BURDENS, NOT PRAYING AT THE DEVIL!

Dick Eastman, a contemporary elder statesman of prayer, has said that "prayer isn't so much another weapon on our list of weaponry as it is the battle itself. It is the arena of conflict in which we engage our enemy."[1] How true! Satan fears prayer and seeks to stop it before it even starts. That shouldn't scare you off, but stir you up all the more. Intercession sounds so super-spiritual, doesn't it? But you can learn the skills of powerful praying.

The Old Testament model. In the old covenant, the intercessor was called to mediate the grace and mercy of the Lord to his chosen people. Sensing both the uncompromising righteousness of God's character and the unrighteousness of human character, this mediator longed for God to receive glory and humankind to receive blessing. When the covenant relationship had become strained, the intercessor longed for God to restore his favor. He or she stood in the gap to plead for forgiveness of sins and deliverance from the enemy's scorn. A survey of various Scriptures details the approach typically followed by the Old Testament intercessor:

- sought the favor of the Lord (Ex 32:22; Dn 9:13-17)
- exalted God's righteousness (Neh 9:5; Dn 9:7)
- reminded God of his promises (Ex 32:13; Ps 85:1-8)
- led out in confession and pleas for mercy (Ex 32:31-32; Neh 9:16-18)

In addition, the intercessor in the old covenant prayed for deliverance from and judgment on the enemy oppressor so that Israel could again proclaim the praises of her God (Neh 9:27-28; Is 64:1-2). Scripture does not paint a picture of the intercessor "praying against" Israel's enemies. Rather, God's power was invoked to judge enemies in his sovereign strength (2 Chr 20; Ps 18:16-19). As David prayed: "Declare them guilty, O God! Let their intrigues be their downfall. Banish them for their many sins, for they have rebelled against you" (Ps 5:10).

New Testament intercession: the view from the cross. Much of Old Testament intercession focuses on confessing sin, seeking forgiveness and favor, and asking for deliverance from enemy oppression. Intercession in the New Testament is significantly different. Modeled most clearly by Paul, our prayers are based on the historical fact of God's favor in the atonement of Christ.

In the shadow of the cross, the intercessory burden is essentially a petition for specific persons to appropriate the favor and fullness of the Father already given through the death and resurrection of the Son.

We must understand the two distinct dimensions to strategic intercession. The first is Godward—reception of direction and instruction from Jesus Christ. The second dimension is satanward—resistance rooted in authority, activated by prayer and empowered by scriptural truth.

Paul prays from the perspective of praise and thanksgiving for the victory already accomplished over sin and Satan. In the first chapter of Ephesians, he praises God "who *has* blessed us," who "*chose* us," and who "*made known* to us the mystery of his will." Then he prays for his fellow believers to know the reality of Jesus' person and the release of his power in their lives (Eph 1:17-19). He's saying in effect, "The greatest event in history has happened. Get the full benefit!"

Can you see and feel Paul's burden in this prayer? Have you ever felt it for someone? This kind of spiritual warfare starts with being in touch with the throne of God. A lifestyle of regular prayer is enhanced by learning to breathe *in* the Spirit's ministry of peace and empowerment (Phil 4:6-7). Then we breathe *out* petitions and praise (Eph 5:19-20).

The resistance to evil we feel is not itself "prayer." It is encounter, engagement, and enforcement of the divine will. We do not "pray" at the devil. We resist him with an authority that comes out of the prayer closet. And we defeat him with heavenly weapons. It is appropriate to remind the devil who he is and where he can go. Let me give you an example of this sort of statement: *I remind you, Satan, that Jesus came to destroy your works. I expose your work in this church. I deny you further access and serve you notice that divine light is penetrating your darkness. The healing of relationships here is closing the door on your influence. You are defeated. Jesus is Victor!*

I have become increasingly uncomfortable in prayer meetings when I see people at one moment engaging in deep prayer to

God, and at the next moment shouting at the devil or some presumed principality. Yes, we can *talk* to the devil and remind him of his certain defeat. But let's be careful to separate our "resistance" of evil from the most holy privilege of *prayer*. It is through prayer that the Lord quickens in us the authority and bold faith to resist and overcome the devil.

CHECKPOINTS IN PREPARATION

Let's assume you find yourself being stirred with other believers toward involvement in strategic prayer. You may feel stirred to establish a "sub-headquarters" of God's kingdom on this wayward earth. A passion grows within you to pray "thy kingdom come" in *your* city! What needs to be happening? What ingredients need to be in place? In my first book, *The Believer's Guide to Spiritual Warfare*, I shared a simple model for beginning strategic warfare. I don't want to duplicate that content, but it would be helpful to review some key points of preparation.

The churches in your locality should show some evidence of God's sovereign stirring across denominational lines to pray for revival in the church and redemption of the lost. This kind of evangelistic hunger can emerge at the grassroots level among the laity or perhaps on a college campus. But ideally it will break forth among those in leadership responsibility. The raising up of pastors and para-church leaders with a passion for prayer is critical.

These "city elders" must share a common experience of Jesus' lordship over the church and the presence of his Spirit in seasons of regular prayer and praise. The Holy Spirit will guide them collectively to ask the question, "What is the kingdom of God to look like here? What is the Lord's heart for our city?"

God waits for us to love and honor one another by giving up our theological pride and petty judgments. He alone can bring unity out of our brokenness. If you're a lay person burdened for your city, plead with God to move in this way in the hearts of both leaders and lay people.

For those involved in strategic intercession, be sure to check out your "perimeters of protection." The following practice of protecting perimeters is a central part of the city-taking model that is followed in Argentina.

Picture four concentric circles, beginning with your own devotional life. Are you entering battle with clean hands and conscience? Do you need to deal with personal strongholds?

The second circle is your marriage and family life. Is your marriage relationship healthy and growing? Peter is bold to say that if a man is insensitive to or neglectful of the needs of his wife, his prayers will be "hindered" (1 Pt 3:7). I believe the same is true for wives. Are you attentive to and praying for your spouse? Are you covering your children by your own obedience and concerted prayers for them?

The third perimeter encompasses working relationships within your ministry or area of service. Have you experienced tension, misunderstanding, unforgiveness, competition, or jealousy among any people on your ministry team? If so, you must all work toward some resolution. Why? Because when you move ahead to penetrate Satan's territory, the hordes of hell will launch a counteroffensive to hit the weak links in the operation. Patch the perimeters. Seal the cracks.

Finally, the fourth perimeter: ensure the harmony of relationships between local church members and leaders. This can be tough. Laity may need to deal with underlying resentment and distrust. Pastors may need to face and resolve longstanding issues, personality conflicts, and competition.

Don't press into battle without checking these perimeters. Conditions will never be perfect or "just right," but do your best to cover the bases. In light of the book of Ephesians, God is preeminently concerned with the quality of our relationships. It is out of corporate unity, cleansed of our sinfulness, that we find strength to stand against the enemy.

What are the cultural, economic, religious, and racial foundations of your town or city? Ask God to raise up someone who has a burden to research the origins of your city. You need this information to move in directions of reconciliation between groups that are alienated from one another.

I have been doing some consulting work with two adjacent, neighboring cities in the Northwest whose churches have undergone enormous tension for decades. It turns out that one city was planned by a logging company as a residence for the "white collar" management types; the other city was intended for the "blue collar" laborers. These cities had been intentionally founded on pride and economic discrimination! No wonder the dream of spiritual unity among the churches had been a nightmare!

What aspects of human sin have given place to enemy control in your area? Does greed, sensuality, violence, racial hatred, murdering of innocents, or the practice of witchcraft pertain to the past history of this place? Someone needs to ask these kinds of questions and provide some discerning analysis. Begin by doing some digging in the county historical library or by talking to the "old-timers" in your town. If God's kingdom is to come in this place, Spirit-led research will uncover strongholds that can be targeted by focused prayer.

People need focal points: prayer and praise events are a necessary ingredient for the success of strategic prayer. The organizers of this prayer effort must elevate the vision and declare their perceptions of what God is doing. In some cities, such a movement begins among the pastors. In others, a key layman or laywoman takes the lead.

God is using hearts that burn *for* him and hands available *to* him. A clear statement of a heaven-sent vision, anointed by the Spirit, will quicken and challenge the local troops. In cooperative concerts of prayer, praise gatherings, or marches, the intercession that emerges can push back the darkness and gain ground in the heavenlies. We may not see any kingdom advancement or be able to measure it, but simple obedience of the body of Christ to abide in love and lift praise to God pleases him and compels him to strike a blow against the enemy.

Willing hands must be trained for battle. Training must be provided for those who want to serve in the Lord's army. While many of the models I share are "leader-driven," initiative can come from anyone. I recently conducted a spiritual warfare seminar for a non-denominational church in Portland. Originally, I was contacted to share just with the women of the church. But the woman in charge had a burden to invite the whole church so that they could be mobilized for prayer. Over three hundred people turned out for a great Saturday seminar! In another Oregon city, a retired layman who has earned the trust of the local churches is plugging them into the prayer movement. These are days of preparation and training. Let's take full advantage of them.

Turn loose local teachers or bring in veterans who can equip the saints in the skills of prayer, spiritual warfare, and evangelism. Assess what is needed to prepare for battle and move toward providing it. Topics could include basic teaching on worship, prayer, spiritual warfare, missions, marriage and family needs. As you consider reaching your area with the gospel, ask the question, "How can we bring the word of life to the people of this city in the most relevant way?" Ask and expect the Lord to reveal outreach strategies that will be especially effective for the people in your locality.

*We need to realize that hurting people turned off
by the church are not going to come to us.
We must be compelled by Jesus' compassion to bring him
to those who are hungry for the bread of life.*

In order to touch the soul of our culture and demonstrate the reality of our faith, we must meet the felt needs of our city. Let me touch on one last element that is such a powerful part of strategic warfare. I almost hesitate to mention it so briefly. Scripture calls this imperative ingredient the "doing of justice" (Mi

6:8), the incarnating of love, putting substance to our spirituality. This means caring about people and their needs, apart from whether they come to Christ or not.

Such efforts may center around providing crisis pregnancy counseling, shelter for women and children fleeing from abusive environments, getting food to the poor, working to resolve racial bigotry, funding and managing drug rehabilitation programs for young people, or providing quality and affordable counseling to people who have been emotionally scarred by dysfunctional families.

What does this sort of outreach have to do with spiritual warfare and evangelism? Plenty! This is what "thy kingdom come" is supposed to look like. We need to realize that hurting people turned off by the church are not going to come to us. We must be compelled by Jesus' compassion to bring him to those who are hungry for the bread of life.

When we have courage and faith to move into the midst of the human mess, to carry even a little matchlight into a dark corner of human degradation, we come against the destroyer. We expose the institutional evil propagated by demonic powers to rob people of simple human dignity. May God give visionary faith and courage to his people to embody the love of his Son to a needy world.

SOME HELPS ON *HOW* TO PRAY

No doubt some of you are already asking, *how* do I pray strategically? Let me offer some direction. Frankly, *the most helpful "help" is the regular practice of worship, seeking, and blessing God for the beauty and majesty of his own being*. We exist to give honor and glory to the King. As we worship, the Lord comes to us. In his presence, we find courage for the battle and wisdom in how to wage it. King Jehoshaphat's response to a massive military threat teaches us a crucial lesson: when worship is an act of total trust in the Almighty, the battle is God's and he handles the enemy (see 2 Chr 20).

I have devoted an earlier chapter to *the necessity of hearing from heaven.* Anyone called to this level of prayer must learn to wait, to cultivate what David Bryant calls a "strategy of silence." Will we choose to slow down long enough, and quiet our own thoughts so we can hear instruction? Schemes, dreams, and "big doings" can entice the flesh to fling itself into a crusade for God that ends up crashing on the rocks of futility. Let's learn to wait, watch, and move in response to a clear word from him.

Prayer warfare is not for the untested (1 Ti 3:1-7). If you are led to this level of involvement, you must be a man or woman of integrity, submitted to authority in a local church. "Loose cannons," independent and immature, do the kingdom more harm than good. It's also dangerous. Unseasoned soldiers are easily stung by satanic hornets stirred up by impulsive efforts.

I know of some well-intended missionaries in Taiwan who acted on impulse to pass out leaflets during a Chinese "ghost festival." They hadn't prayed much about it and didn't pray for it. They just hit the streets. The spiritual "kickback" of oppression and strife within their own ranks was enormous. They learned the hard way.

We must keep the redemption of people always clearly in focus (Lk 10:20; 1 Ti 2:1-6). Spiritual warfare endeavors that do not result in people coming into the kingdom are a waste of time and effort.

We must maintain a high view of God's sovereignty over evil (Jb 42:2). This isn't always easy. Sometimes it seems the devil is winning and the reinforcements have been cut off at the pass. The prayer warrior must choose to affirm the goodness and sovereignty of God in the face of apparent failure. Even when we wrestle with perplexity, we should press on with Paul's assurance that God is the blessed controller of all circumstances (Rom 8:28-29).

As I mentioned above in my comments about preparation, certain elements are key to God's hearing and answering "thy kingdom come" kinds of prayers. *Participants must be unified and in right relationship to one another* (Acts 4:32), having been cleansed of unforgiveness (Mk 11:25) and sharing a consensual agreement in the authority of Jesus. They must agree together that what they are asking is of the Lord and honoring to him (Mt 18:19-20). We don't need to guess at God's mind. His Spirit can guide us to agree on a sure word. Such agreement on the written Word in prayer on behalf of a person, situation, or city holds great power.

Those who come together for such kingdom praying must also possess strong, unwavering faith. They need the ability to envision God's answer, with one eye fixed on eternity and the other fixed on the human need (Rom 4:20-21). Those who are called to dig into prayer at this level will also find that *perseverance through persecution and oppressive counterattack is imperative* (Rom 5:3-5; 2 Cor 4:7-12). Such perseverance requires proven, Christlike character, a tenacity born out of the crucible of crisis and pressure.

Our Captain will provide us with sufficient exposure to real battle for us to learn how to handle the heat and remain firm in our faith. Many times God allows Satan to buffet the would-be warrior. Even though painful and perplexing, such seasoning of character and sharpening of skills can come no other way.

SHARPENING OUR PRAYER POINTS: *WHAT* TO PRAY

All skilled warriors know how to use their weapons. The Lord is looking for men and women of faith willing to learn how to pray strategically. But *what* precisely do we pray? What does this kind of praying look and sound like? I offer the following points of prayer as suggested "arrows in the quiver," merely a sampling, surely not meant to be comprehensive. Biased towards evangelistic praying, these suggestions are presented under three separate categories: prayers for the church generally, for Christian workers specifically, and for the unsaved. In the next section, we'll consider various styles of prayer.

For the church:
- For individuals and particular churches to return to Jesus as their first love, to have a passion for his presence, and to please him in every respect (Rv 2:4-5; 3:20).
- For an organic unity among Christians, based on common love for and life in Jesus Christ. Unity validates the reality; reality opens doors for harvest (Jn 17:23; Eph 4:3-6).
- For exposure of strongholds within the church that hinder revival and give Satan advantage, e.g., criticism, pride, unbelief, or the idolatries of sensuality and materialism (Jas 3:13-4:7; 1 Jn 2:15-17).
- That fellow Christians would be open to take on and enter into the redemptive burdens of God's heart; that more believers would be gripped by the Lord's compassion for the lost (2 Cor 5:11-21).
- That God would be pleased to begin and sustain a movement of prayer in our town or city; that he would raise a people committed to prevail in prayer until the local church is revived (Is 62:6-7; Ps 85:1-8).

For Christian workers:
- That Jesus, the Lord of the harvest, would speak to and send out workers to reap the current harvest, especially young people in college, early retirees, and occupational tentmakers (Mt 9:35-38).
- For strengthening of the hearts (encouragement) and hands (equipping) of pastors, missionaries, evangelists, and disciplers involved in the harvest (Col 1:9-11; 2 Thes 1:11, 12).
- For divine protection from satanic schemes that would discourage and diminish effectiveness in service; for a shield around the family, for the power of the blood of Christ to cover his workers, for the ministry of the angels to come to their aid (Ps 91; Jn 17:15; 2 Thes 3:3).
- That the word spoken through these servants would be anointed by the power of the Holy Spirit to penetrate demonic darkness, pierce hearts with conviction, and bring men and women to faith (Eph 6:19-20; Col 4:2-6; Acts 10:34-44).

For the unsaved:

- For a release of the presence and power of the Holy Spirit to convict individuals of "guilt in regard to sin and righteousness and judgment" (Jn 16:8); for the Spirit to bring a healthy guilt in the face of judgment.
- For particular persons, that God would actively "open their eyes and turn them from darkness to light, and from the power of Satan to God, so that they may receive forgiveness of sins" (Acts 26:18).
- For subduing and separating the influence of evil spirits from the mind, will, and emotions of these individuals, while standing on Jesus' word that in building his church, "the gates of Hades will not overcome it" (Mt 16:18).
- For the felt needs of this person—e.g., loneliness, employment, marriage problems, financial needs, comfort in medical tragedy, a wayward child—that the Lord would meet those needs as a validation of his personal care. Offer to pray for the human needs of unsaved friends and acquaintances, giving the Lord an opportunity to demonstrate his compassion.
- Offer short, spontaneous petitions in the midst of daily contacts, such as, "Lord, raise up more workers to reach these young people." Or "Open a door of conversation with this person." Or "Jesus, I claim John for salvation in the authority of your name." The power of these prayers lies in the sincerity of your compassion and the strength of your faith.
- For the Lord to sovereignly use the pressure of circumstances to compel a person toward conviction and seeking, perhaps personal circumstances such as a failed relationship, an accident, a financial loss, a health problem. You are praying, "Lord, bring John to the end of himself. Get his attention." Natural calamities, wars, and economic upheaval serve as powerful catalysts. Increased interest in spiritual things became evident during the Persian Gulf War, after the earthquake in the San Francisco Bay area, and in the aftermath of Hurricane Andrew in Florida.
- For conversions that are "sound" (solid, sincere, lasting)

and "significant" (persons of influence—leaders, athletes, secular humanists, scientists) that the harvest may be multiplied.

- As guided by the Spirit, for the weakening of territorial strongholds of evil that hinder acceptance of the gospel, e.g., greed, sensuality, intellectual cynicism, witchcraft.
- For a particular nation or people group, regularly and systematically bringing to the Lord all of the prayer points above. Choose to make this a long-term investment prayer, believing the Lord to be penetrating the darkness with the light of his Word and the lives of his workers in that nation.

These are just a few "prayer points" to guide your strategic intercession for the building of the church. Be sure to keep uppermost in mind the lack of any magic or prayer formula that assures success. In this warfare for the destiny of souls, people are won for the most part through personal contact, one by one. And once won, each person must be built up to be a productive member of the body. I'm convinced that the Lord is applying pressure on our world and opening doors for greater harvest. Now is the time to sit in his school of learning and prepare to pray people out of darkness into the light of his kingdom.

MAKING NEW HABITS: *WAYS* TO PRAY

Let's explore some of the various ways to participate in strategic prayer. At its core, life is a "push-pull" struggle. The pull of self-centeredness, sin, and satanic deception often seems overwhelming. If we apply the physical law of inertia to the spiritual world, we understand that it takes a compelling power from God to turn a person's eyes heavenward. As the Lord of the harvest continues to call people into the church, let's commit ourselves to pray more concertedly and precisely for particular persons. I want to focus here on specific intercession formats that move God's heart to touch the lives of those who don't yet know him.

Personal Closet Praying. Each one of us is individually responsible for cultivating our own personal prayer life. How many of you know what a huge challenge this can be? The gap between what we know we ought to do and what we really do can be quite wide. While we can often be consumed just praying for our families and friends, we must remember that God is eager to answer prayers offered for every single one of his lost sheep.

If we are going to become personally motivated to pray for the lost sheep of this world, the pain and misery of human suffering must get through to us.

Can we dare to ask the Lord to give us his burdens? As we watch news reports on crises in other lands and see faces and hear agonized cries, are we prompted to pray for people groups and nations? In light of the reality of judgment, can we look at others with an eye of compassion, knowing that they may face the horrors of hell? If we are going to become personally motivated to pray for the lost sheep of this world, the pain and misery of human suffering must get through to us. Take advantage of an opportunity to become better acquainted with someone from another nation. Walk through the corridors of a local high school over the lunch hour. Visit an ethnic or economically poor church. Be willing to feel God's heartbeat.

To focus my own efforts toward intercession, I keep a simple prayer journal divided into six sections: personal and family needs; mutual requests that my wife and I pray about together; Christian friends and acquaintances; Christian workers and ministries; government leaders; and unsaved individuals, people groups, and nations. On the left side of the page I list each intention, and on the right side write dates and comments as to how and when the Lord is answering.

I carry this prayer journal with me, allowing the Holy Spirit to expand it as he wills. I'm not legalistic or overly compulsive about when and how long I pray through the journal; otherwise, I would doom myself to failure. Yet the discipline of a tangible, written journal has spurred me on. It objectifies the thoughts and promptings that might otherwise seem ethereal. Increasingly, I have been drawn to pray for particular unreached nations and those ministries which target them.

Since I travel a great deal, I rest my journal on the dashboard of my car en route to airports. Often in the idle moments before take off, I will pray through a section or two. My office is near some woods, so I have developed a habit of walking into the woods for fifteen minutes, lifting up names of those whom I am trusting to the Lord.

If you really want the Lord to change your personal prayer habits, I challenge you to fast a meal or two. Ask God specifically to increase your discipline, perhaps devoting a breakfast and lunch hour to such a focus. Take a partial or a full day to go to a quiet place with just your Bible, a devotional book, and your journal. Let God guide you into prayer that goes beyond obligatory duty and drudgery. Let him make these times in his presence and seasons of petition a special delight.

Prayer-partnering. Joining together with another brother or sister in a prayer partnership can both increase your discipline to pray and encourage your faith. Jesus promises that if two or three agree on something of concern to him, that he is present in our midst and will answer (Mt 18:18-20). Can we take him at his word?

Prayer-partnering is so powerful, yet so neglected. The chemistry has to be right. Have you noticed certain persons with whom you seem to click spiritually? It might be a friend you've known for years or it might be a new acquaintance. But your spirits are in harmony. You share a common motivation and vision; you experience Jesus' presence when you pray.

Frankly, I believe this kind of joint prayer between marriage partners to be one of the greatest untapped prayer reservoirs in the church. I remember one evening years ago when I took the time to initiate an evening of prayer with Terri. As the Lord brought us deeper into his presence, it seemed that his Spirit was saying, "More, ask me for more… just ask." God was greatly pleased with our partnership and has proven many times since that he hears and answers.

As a single person or parent, you can experience the very same blessing. Ask God to lead you to a person with whom you can comfortably pray. I highly recommend one particular book as especially inspiring and instructional in this regard, *Two Are Better than One,* authored by David Mains.[2] He shares forms and focuses which would fit any partner-prayer relationship.

The prayer cell. The prayer cell typically consists of any group that meets regularly together, often combined with other purposes such as a Bible study, discipleship group, a church leadership committee, elders or deacons, a Moms in Touch group, a neighborhood women's fellowship, or even lunch-hour interaction at work. When the chemistry is right, such groups can be conducive for deeper prayers of agreement.

Many Christians begin by praying for one another's needs, or for their families and friends. If your group efforts are to be broadened, someone needs to take leadership to articulate the priority of praying for unsaved persons. Such a leader might simply challenge the group members in their prayer time to honestly ask God to share his heart burdens with them.

I believe these prayer cells can assume some kind of geographical responsibility. A men's prayer group at a plant could pray for other workers. The neighborhood women's fellowship could pray for local families. A home Bible study could be led to pray regularly for specific neighbors. A group could literally put feet to its praying by walking around a place of employment or a neighborhood and letting the Holy Spirit guide and prompt petitions.

Clear leadership can help direct and target the focus of such a group. I recently visited a rapidly growing church in Phoenix which has a full-time minister of prayer. At the time of my visit, each of their prayer cells kept names of unsaved persons written on colored pieces of paper. All these had been collected, then individually prayed over by the church intercessory team, stapled together in a chain, and strung around the perimeter of the sanctuary. This church also practices regular outreach to non-Christians that meets distinct needs. I believe cell group prayer is the key to its rapid growth.

The Christian family has enormous potential to practice this kind of prayer. In addition to regular times of worship and prayer at home, we can mark out special times to lift up the "hundredth sheep" to the Father. Dads can focus on fellow employees, supervisors, or work contacts. Moms can pray for other mothers or contacts at work.

Kids in our "me-centered" culture need to experience God's heart for the lost and be discipled in "other-centered" prayer. We can challenge our children to choose one or two friends at school and to believe God for their salvation. A family can adopt a child in another culture through a sponsoring program or choose a nation to pray for regularly. Profiles of unreached people groups and nations are being made available today which offer excellent information and visual focus for prayer.

ANOTHER STYLE OF PRAYER: "FAITH WALKS"

It is one thing to sit in a room with fellow believers and try to visualize a place or city for which you are praying. Visual and interactive contact adds a fresh dimension to the work of those watching over the city walls. The Lord has for some time now been prompting men and women to engage in what have become known as "faith walks." Some have called this style of prayer "Joshua" or "Jericho" walks.

Faith walking simply incorporates praying on-site with inspired insight, listening for the voice of God concerning his will for a particular place. Faith walking is an act that frankly sometimes feels a bit foolish, but if rightly motivated demonstrates faith and authority. We please God by demonstrating our confidence that he is at work. As believers burdened for a people or a city or a nation, we need mutual encouragement. Faith walking provides an opportunity for us to become visible to one another. Surely we are already visible to the hidden hosts of hell and heaven, those spiritual powers who wage war behind the scenes of normal everyday life.

Faith walking can increase our potential to change the spiritual atmosphere of a particular place by our presence and petitions. While actively walking and watching, we pay attention to waiting on God for revelation and instruction. We try to engage in relevant, on-target prayers. At points the waiting may turn to warring in the power of the Spirit, fervent prayer that is focused on weakening particular strongholds. Though the particular methods of this style of praying vary, the movement is gaining momentum.

When the Lord opened Abram's eyes of faith and offered him an inheritance, he told him, "Go, walk through the length and breadth of the land, for I am giving it to you" (Gn 13:17). We dare not pull this divine promise out of Scripture and put ourselves in the place of Abram. God spoke this specific word to him concerning the whole plan of redemption. But I am interested in the principle of walking about the land where God has placed us and claiming it for his purposes.

The psalmist declared, "The scepter of the wicked will not remain over the land allotted to the righteous" (Ps 125:3). Can we stand on this promise as we seek to manifest the kingdom in our towns and cities? I believe so. The authority of evil individuals and institutions must be challenged with a higher authority.

We see that the removal of spiritual pollution was common in Old Testament times. Moses instructed Israel: "Destroy completely all the places on the high mountains and on the hills ... where the nations you are dispossessing worship their gods.... Cut down the idols of their gods and wipe out their names from those places" (Dt 12:2-3). Josiah, a man of righteousness, came on the scene and set about ridding the land of elements of desecration (see 2 Kgs 23). Josiah acted as an intercessor by taking visible and verbal authority over evil.

Certain "high places" in our land are unholy, dark corners in our cities that keep doors open to the demonic hosts. Many times I have led prayer walks to such high places—shrines, New Age bookstores, pornography shops, university campuses, town halls, courthouses, headquarters of occult organizations. I have often experienced the strange tension between following a prompting that is pleasing to God and feeling the resistance of hell in leading such an offensive charge.

*I am not advocating a zealous, simplistic crusade
to drive devils out of our towns.
Prayer walking is not for the immature or improperly motivated,
but for those called and burdened to pray for the fulfillment
of God's kingdom purposes in a particular place.*

I do not believe these styles of praying should be viewed as Christian grandstanding. I am not advocating a zealous, simplistic crusade to drive devils out of our towns. Prayer walking is not for the immature or improperly motivated, but for those called and burdened to pray for the fulfillment of God's kingdom purposes in a particular place.

We must always center on our responsibility to share the good news. Be open to the creativity of the Holy Spirit. In my own city, a woman devised a plan for local intercessors to pray up and down every street in town. In Toronto, a small prayer group pursued a vision for Christians to pray through the city telephone white pages, name by name. Enough intercessors came to a special prayer meeting in the Skydome to designate one page per praying person!

Success comes out of a silent waiting for the Lord's signals; its strength is born in worship and praise that precedes the petitioning. A strong, Spirit-led leader is essential, someone who can offer clear instruction as to what to expect and what the prayer warriors aim to accomplish. Let me share with you some of the elements of prayer walking that I have learned over the years.

Preparation. Please don't just jump into a prayer walk. You should thoughtfully identify prayer targets and concerns beforehand. You could focus on prayers of blessing for churches and ministers or prayers asking God to penetrate strongholds. Challenge participants to seek the Lord in quiet times for Scriptures that relate to your location.

Carefully "put on the full armor of God" (Eph 6:11) to assure protection from any enemy counterattacks. I have found demonic resistance to this kind of planned prayer walk to be subtle but strong. Explain that you are pursuing three distinct goals: gathering information on enemy strongholds; perceiving God's heart for this city; and learning to pray strategically. Expect the Lord to inspire and lead you to offer prayers of investment in the work of his kingdom. Fasting before and during the event is encouraged.

Initial prayer. Commit the walk to the Lord as you begin. While there is certainly no "right" way to do this, you should cover some necessary bases. With praise and thanksgiving, claim the protection and assurances of Psalm 91. Invite the Spirit of God to envelope your group as a shield. Explain openly that this endeavor is likely to provoke some demonic attention. Lift together the shield of faith that has power to extinguish the enemy's arrows. Petition God to give you his heart for your city. Praying for a place or people you do not love strikes me as both difficult and inappropriate. Let God plant his burdens in your heart. Pray for discernment, for the ability to see your community with spiritual eyes.

Making plans. You might ask, how exactly do I do this? Sometimes I have had people meet first at a local church, a city park, or someone's home for preparatory prayer. Then you can break into van-loads and drive to the four compass points of the city, with four groups walking and praying toward the center of the city. If your town has an identifiable and manageable border, you might all want to march around the perimeter, moving in clusters of four or five.

Often we have chosen target areas and assigned a group to each one for an hour of intercession. These days, certain places are sometimes known to be used by occultists, witches, or satanists. This may literally be a high place, a hilltop or nearby mountain. It might be a local park, even a graveyard. If you can, develop rapport with your local police department to obtain this information. In larger cities, you can caravan from place to place or drive the perimeter of a town. Be creative. Follow the Lord's lead.

Identifying prayer targets. On the positive side, identify churches and pastors or para-church organizations to bless with your prayers. Again, let the Scriptures keep you on track. When praying for key pastors in a city, I like Paul's apostolic prayers.[3] Pray for a release of the Spirit's presence in the worship services and God's anointing on the messages of local pastors.

In light of the Lord's promise to protect us from evil (2 Thes 3:3), you might also pray for a breaking of curses spoken against the Christian leaders and their families. A Baptist pastor called just the other day asking for such prayer. He serves as point man in an effort to block a major New Age group from establishing a training center for teenagers in their town on the Oregon coast. This pastor had been besieged with threatening phone calls and harassment, unfortunately part of today's spiritual situation.

On the negative side, ask God to show you what you're really up against in your town, perhaps in the form of a spiritual stronghold or an actual place or organization. You will begin to perceive the presence of wider or larger cultural strongholds, such as greed, idolatry of self, and sensuality. Look for local evidences of enemy activity particular to your city, e.g., crack houses used to manufacture drugs, high occurrence of teen suicide or domestic violence, the frequency of particular crimes, or the presence of an organization committed to New Age teachings.

In choosing locations in which to physically plant your feet, consider walking around a university campus, city government buildings, churches of a more liberal persuasion, or corporate business entities that have power and profile in the community. Let God guide you as to "what to pray" in these places (see above).

Repentance and redemption. Remember, you cannot expect to magically or instantly pray either human sinfulness or satanic influence out of your city. The primary focus of prayer must be for repentance among God's people that brings revival, and for conviction of the unsaved concerning the reality of sin and judgment.

The church today is so polluted by societal sin,
that the intercessor must prevail in asking God to draw us
back to purity in his presence.

As intercessors watching over our cities, we may be led to repent of the sins of the city, both for the church and for the unsaved. We can follow the models of Daniel and Nehemiah who pleaded with God for mercy to forgive the sins of the people and to restore their ability to proclaim God's praise. The church today is so polluted by societal sin that the intercessor must prevail in asking God to draw us back to purity in his presence.

While walking, target specific groups of people who need to know the Lord, like youth, athletes, career professionals, university professors, or government officials. Release the power of the Holy Spirit to bring conviction. When you are on-site praying with insight, the Spirit of God will guide your petitions.

Recently at one of my seminars I met several bold young men and women with a vision to plant a church in West Los Angeles, near Hollywood. The local populace predominantly worships the lust of the eyes, the lust of the flesh, and the pride of life. But these young warriors dress like the locals, walk the streets, make contact, build relationships, and pray for the kingdom to come in that place.

Debriefing. Whatever way your group chooses to pray on-site, it is important to conclude your walk with a debriefing session. You need to share impressions, gather your insights, and encourage each other. Many times I have sensed that people felt nothing had been accomplished during the prayer walk. We so easily fall prey to our natural methods of measurement and lose heart. Because warfare is involved, exhaustion and discouragement can set in. The leader must keep the larger, long-term picture clearly in focus. He or she can remind the participants that their prayers will add weight to those petitions already offered up for that city over the years.

Big faith demands a big vision of God, along with patience to wait for the fulfillment of his purposes. Encourage your group to share any thoughts and feelings. Sometimes what seems like a mere subjective impression will resonate with another person and find confirmation. What did you feel as we walked around the pornography shop? What went through your mind when we walked through the capitol building? What did you sense God wanting to do in our city? Take note of these responses and build corporate discernment.

When you poke a stick into the hornet's nest, someone might get harassed, even stung. Expect this as a part of the turf of strategic warfare.

Watch for counterattack. The devil is certainly not fond of fired-up Christians pressing in and praying around his perimeter of power. When you poke a stick into the hornet's nest, someone might get harassed, even stung. Expect this kind of counterattack as a part of the turf of strategic warfare. Don't be surprised by fiery trials. Don't panic if someone gets sick, or has an auto accident, or an unusual difficulty with a child. Don't think it unusual if a situation blows up in your church.

The devil will naturally try to scare us away from strategic prayer. Stay the course. Hold steady with the sure Word of Scripture: "The reason the Son of God appeared was to destroy the devil's work" (1 Jn 3:8). Take a helpful hint from James: "Consider it pure joy, my brothers, whenever you face trials of many kinds, because you know that the testing of your faith develops perseverance" (Jas 1:2-3).

Our God allows Satan to push us back in order to force our dependence upon God himself and to toughen our faith. As prayer warriors, we must learn to praise God in our pain and perplexities, to trust him through our trials. If we respond without fear, walking in the Spirit and praying for one another, Satan's counterattacks will blow up in his own face.

HOW SHOULD WE PRAY AT EVANGELISTIC EVENTS?

Have you ever found yourself at an event where the gospel was being presented to non-Christians? Do you find yourself wondering how to pray more effectively? I sure do. I feel the weight of the moment, but fumble to know precisely how to point my prayers.

As members of the prayer committee for the Billy Graham Crusade in Portland, Oregon, we were given a special glass-enclosed room at the Civic Stadium which directly overlooked the seats and field below. For each crusade event, we led local intercessors in prayers for empowerment of Dr. Graham, anointing of the word, binding of enemy influence, and outpouring of the Spirit.

Every service was different. As ministers, homemakers, laypeople, and students committed to strategic prayer, we sought the mind of Jesus to guide us. It was my turn to lead this intercessory prayer group one evening. Walking on the playing field while the crowd was still gathering, I sensed an intense restlessness— like I was in the middle of a spiritual wrestling match. And that's precisely what that evening's service turned out to be.

The police command post was located adjacent to the prayer

room. They were searching for a man who had made a death threat on Dr. Graham. A youth packing a gun had been reported. The scriptural message that evening from Jonah was powerfully pointed: a challenge to the city of Portland to repent, from the upper echelons of society on down. As leader of a little pack of praying people, I felt as never before the intensity of wrestling for the souls of men, women, and children. The Lord led us to subdue, on the spot, the blinding work of the enemy. At the invitation people streamed toward the field to receive Christ.

I asked Dr. Graham the next night to share his impressions on the Portland Crusade in general. He immediately referred to the night before, saying that he had never experienced such intense wrestling. Dr. Graham felt as if the devil were challenging him at every point of his message. True evangelism is spiritual warfare.

Whether at an evangelistic crusade, a men's breakfast, a Sunday morning service, a youth outreach, or a neighborhood event for children, let's learn to pray with bold authority to silence the voice of the enemy and subdue his power. Let's pierce through the demonic smoke screen that blinds people from seeing Jesus as he is. Let's pray for a release of the Holy Spirit to compel the lost to decide to be found by the One who searches for their hearts.

SPECIAL DAYS AND EVENTS

Practitioners of witchcraft and satanism are committed to observing certain "unholy" days, like Halloween, the solstice, and equinox dates of seasonal transition. Former occultists have told me that on some of these occasions, they engage in ritual cursings of Christian leaders, their families, and churches.

In many communities today, church groups often host alternative "Harvest" parties for families, as well as meetings for celebrative praise and focused prayer against the things of darkness. We need to be aware of the formal satanic calendar and mobilize both defensive and offensive prayer on these dates: February 2, March 20 (spring equinox), April 26-May 1, June 21 (summer solstice), August 3, September 22 (fall equinox), October 29-November 1 (All Hallow's Eve), and December 22-24 (winter solstice). My counseling data has confirmed many times over that ritualistic sacrifices—animal and human—occur particularly during these times. Should we not take initiative at these times to intercede? Can we not be pro-active in piercing darkness?

Easter services boast the highest frequency of annual attendance on the part of nominal and non-Christians. A form of "planting prayer" proves to be especially effective on such occasions. Plant yourself in a congregation and ask the Holy Spirit to guide your prayers for specific persons around you or for types of people in the crowd, such as young moms, professional men and women, or college students. Pray that the word spoken and sung will have power to penetrate the veil of unbelief.

As a prayer warrior in the making, another helpful focus involves watching for cultural or world events that cause fear or uncertainty. Most people only change while under pressure or faced with problems. The Lord uses the calamities of natural, health, and financial disasters to get people's attention. Such trouble can be the point at which a person turns to seek the Lord, or else turns bitter. Let him teach you how to pray while reading a news magazine or watching television news. Learn to petition the Lord to draw hurting, questioning people toward himself.

I've only scratched the surface with these suggestions. My intention is simply to prime your pump and stimulate you to jump in and do it. If we have God's heart and see people as he does, we're never quite the same. May the Lord lead each one of you to apply these principles and practice a new style of authoritative prayer that shakes other people free from the enemy's shackles.

9

Ready for Outpouring

Those whom I love I rebuke and discipline. So be earnest,
and repent. Here I am! I stand at the door and knock.
If anyone hears my voice and opens the door,
I will come in and eat with him, and he with me. **Rv 3:19-20**

JESUS INCLUDED THIS AGONIZED APPEAL in his discourse to the
seven churches in the Revelation to John. He's not address-
ing unbelievers who hear the voice of the Savior for the first time
and open the door of their hearts to a saving relationship. The
Lord speaks here to those who are supposed to know him inti-
mately already!

"Here I am!" Left on the outside of the church looking in,
longing for intimate communion with those he has redeemed,
Jesus is trying to recapture our attention, simply because he
loves us.

Recently at my home church, our pastor shared a sermon
illustration. He had come home one day searching the house for
his preschool son, David. He walked through the upstairs, calling
his name. He looked in various rooms, following a trail of toys.
He decided to look downstairs, calling "Davie, Daddy's home!"

No response. He went to David's room, rapped his knuckles on the door, only to find further signs of wreckage. "David, are you down here son?"

Then he heard some muffled humming noises from the family room. Little David sat on the floor, so engrossed in his pile of Legos that he had either not heard, or just not responded, to his father's calls. Dad quietly stooped over his son. With a gentle touch, he took the boy's chin and turned it upward. Catching his attention with eye contact and a caring voice, Dad addressed his son: "Hi, buddy, how ya doin'?"

What's your Lego pile? What keeps you occupied and preoccupied, distracted from listening for Jesus' voice?

Revelation 3:19-20 reflects just this kind of intimate relationship. Jesus cares enough about us to get our attention. If we don't perceive his presence soon enough, he must resort to rebuke and discipline. He calls us to repent, to open wide the doors of our hearts, to receive our daily bread of deepest communion with him.

What's *your* Lego pile? What keeps *you* occupied and preoccupied, distracted from listening for Jesus' voice? Is it the pursuit of prosperity, an overindulgence in leisure, an addiction to watching athletics, your own job or career, perhaps even your family? Finding the balance between a God-given enjoyment of "normal life" and the call to live first for the kingdom is no easy matter. To what extent are we willing to sacrifice our own desires? The Holy Spirit alone can speak to each one of us and put his finger on our individual idolatries.

What do we need to do to restore the blessing of Jesus' personal presence in his church so we can radiate his reality to an unbelieving world? Many today are experiencing a renewed hunger for spiritual food. Will we let God have his way, mold our thinking, and mentor our ministries? He is crafting something of beauty with his own hands. Let's resolve to leave our human fingerprints off his handiwork. Let's allow Jesus to build the church his way.

GETTING OUR ATTENTION

How incredibly loving Jesus is. In his message to each of the seven churches, he first affirms the good he sees in them (see Rv 1-3). The Lord offers his people unspeakably wonderful promises: to eat of the tree of life, to partake of hidden manna, to hold authority over the nations, to stand as a permanent pillar in God's eternal temple, to sit on the throne with the King!

Jesus fully intends to turn over the kingdom to his chosen ones. Yet the obstacle to this inheritance is our own penchant for sin. In chapters 2 and 3, Jesus isolates the issues: forsaking him as first love, sexual immorality, lifeless religiosity, and self-sufficiency. These sins, along with many others, quench the blessing of the Spirit and shut the Savior out of communion with his beloved. Yet we see reasons for great hope. In his mercy, God is convicting us of our sin, while stirring up in us a craving for him alone.

What evidence of personal renewal can we look for in ourselves? Longing for intimacy with the Lord is the beginning point. When we hunger and thirst for the real Bread of Life, what emerges from this desire is a heartfelt repentance for the "wicked ways" that block the doorway to our hearts. Once we admit our propensity for wrong-doing, we begin to recognize the deeper subtleties of a self that is alive and well: pride, criticism, resentments, self-protection.

Do we dare invite the Lord to strip away our layers of compromise and self-sufficiency? Honestly, where are *you* in your walk with Jesus? Are you hungering and thirsting, or complacent on a safe plateau? Each of us must be willing to say to him, "expose me, forgive me, heal me." In truth, we must exchange our lives for his. No pathway to relational union with Jesus exists apart from a forsaking of self and a full embracing of his life. In this act of dying to ourselves, the depth of pain and the joy of promise meet together. John the Baptist knew the secret: "He must become greater; I must become less" (Jn 3:30).

So why am I talking about this in a book on evangelism? Because I am convinced that we must be about the business of *being* the people of God before becoming pre-occupied with *doing* great things for God. New life must become an integral part of our own being before we can ask others to believe.

By his own sovereign initiative, Jesus is bringing his people into this reality. Those with discernment and understanding can recognize the sovereign stamp of the Almighty on world affairs. The sheer rapidity and intensity in current events boggles the mind. Beyond the veneer of earthly events, what is the Head of the church saying to his body? I believe the following impressions reflect God's heart toward us at this time. If accurate, these thoughts will resonate in you.

Supreme affection for Jesus. Our Father longs for us to fall in love with his Son and fall before him in worship. I have come to see that this is where he wants us, broken and bowed before the throne. The Lord himself prompts a deep longing in our hearts for praise and prayer. When I travel from culture to culture, I am finding the very same hunger for greater spiritual reality.

Jesus is pulling at our hearts, nudging us to individually and corporately invite him in for spiritual fellowship. If this is happening in your heart, pursue his presence. Follow the signals. Take the next step. Agonize over your sin and self-centeredness. But don't stay there long. Seek his forgiveness and abandon yourself to the peace of the Lord's presence:

> Turn your eyes upon Jesus,
> Look full in his wonderful face.
> And the things of earth will grow strangely dim,
> In the light of his glory and grace.[1]

When we fall on our knees before the Lord in worship, we fulfill the very reason for our being, the highest of all life's purposes. In worship, we acknowledge that God is the very source of our life and its meaning, above all other things. Jesus so longs for us to see and to live this truth that he graciously gives us the vision of his glorious throne in Revelation 4 and 5. When we bring him worship, he bestows overflowing blessings.

A reclaiming of the church. In essence, Revelation 2 and 3 reflect Jesus' desire to reclaim what is rightfully his. Gentleman that he is, the Lord asks for that privilege. I believe some churches and organizations will joyfully open the door to him. Others, however, will remain entrenched in a deadening religious traditionalism. Some will view this movement of the Spirit with skepticism, judging it to be another wave of fanaticism. But it is happening too far and wide to be just that.

What I see are scores of evangelicals, charismatics, mainliners, no-liners, born-again Catholics, high church, low church, big church, no church believers sick of their way of doing church and longing only for Jesus.

In the opening of chapter eight, I shared the story of inviting those attending my seminar in Budapest, Hungary, to join me for prayer in a hillside park overlooking the city. All of the participants responded enthusiastically, conservatives and charismatics alike, hungry to please God's heart by agreeing in prayer. The gathering was profound. The petitions were powerful.

The next evening, I was privileged to preach at an experimental service, a joint meeting of a conservative and a charismatic church. As the worship team began to lead and as hands began to gently lift, the tension began to rise in the room. The conservatives sat on the edge of their seats—not in anticipation but in agonized discomfort! I turned around to see the leaders of both churches pacing and praying. *Praise you, Father! Thank you for your presence here. Grace your people with the liberty of your love. Grant us healing from our suspicions and divisions.* Gently but unmistakably, the unifying peace of his presence filled the room. It felt so good to just be counted among the Father's family!

What am I getting at here? A new ecumenism? No. A new world fellowship of non-traditionalist, fervent hearts? Surely not. A doing away with denominations? Not necessarily. What I see are scores of evangelicals, charismatics, mainliners, no-liners, born-again Catholics, high church, low church, big church, no church believers sick of their way of doing church and longing only for Jesus.

Does this sound too idealistic and simplistic? I see it happening. We are witnessing a razing of religious barriers and a raising up of a remnant. Only in the cross does Jesus break down the walls that divide us. Only around the certainty of his sovereign lordship can we rally. Our Lord declared, "When I am lifted up from the earth, [I] will draw all men to myself" (Jn 12:32). We usually interpret this in terms of evangelism. I believe Jesus' words also apply to fellowship among the redeemed. He is bringing us to a conciliatory unity based on common love for himself.

In a unity based on the essentials of biblical faith, we need not compromise the theological convictions connected to our own heritage. We're all going to have to live together in glory. We might try to enjoy some of the flavor of that fellowship now. Theological differences will continue. We will still experience tension over spiritual gifts, sacraments, and interpretations of the Scriptures. Nevertheless, we can choose to love, respect, pray, and praise together. John Wesley, my favorite theologian, summed it up like this: "In things essential, there must be unity. In non-essentials, tolerance. In all things, charity."

If such unity were not possible, Jesus wouldn't have commanded it. We all know the Master's petition in his great priestly prayer: "that all of them may be one, Father, just as you are in me and I am in you. May they also be in us so that the world may believe that you have sent me" (Jn 17:21). Jesus is praying on behalf of "those who will believe in me through [the disciples'] message" (v. 20).

This side of eternity, short of the glory of his presence, is such oneness really possible? Is this a pipe dream or credible reality? Dare we hope for our labels to be removed, our hearts to be bended—our schisms to be healed? Can we realistically hope to enter such reconciliation without compromising our deepest doctrinal convictions? With God, all things are possible.

We will never achieve full doctrinal unity this side of heaven. Too many theological distinctives and polarities block the way. We are nevertheless exhorted to maintain the unity of the Spirit in the bond of peace (Eph 4:1-6). But there is among God's people an insidious stronghold that saps strength from our organic unity. It is *sectarianism*. How can we hope to have God's heart for the lost if our hearts are stony and judgmental toward a brother or sister? For example, evangelicals can identify and forsake their pride about their knowledge of the Bible and "sound" theology. Charismatics can recognize and confess their pride about experiences with the Holy Spirit and worship style.

I believe many Christians long for this unity. In prayer gatherings, I have often heard the quoting of David's lovely words: "How good and pleasant it is when brothers live together in unity!... For there the Lord bestows his blessing" (Ps 133:1-3).

Apart from the occasional cross-denominational prayer meeting or cooperative endeavors in evangelism, can this depth of unity become reality? Is there any way to actually model the organic oneness of the body? The Lord is showing us his way. The believability of Jesus' life and message hangs in the balance. When will we learn to love one another?

As the witness of our oneness becomes more tangible, the world will have greater cause to believe. The unity that centers on the common confession of the Lordship of Christ and agreement on the requirements of saving faith contributes to more effective evangelism. The bonding of agape love exposes and breaks the power of strongholds.

A deepening desire for holiness. A deep desire for holiness doesn't come easily for a people entrenched in the demonic muck of the world system. The church has been suffering from serious toxicity. The purity of our spirituality has been poisoned. Our lifeblood has seeped away into the darkness.

Peter gives it to us straight: "But just as he who called you is holy, so be holy in all you do" (1 Pt 1:15). That's a huge challenge today. But I see increased evidence that God is granting to many of us a heart hunger for holiness. He wants to purify us with the sanctifying grace of his Spirit, if we but yield to him in faith. Pruning is painful, but it produces purity and greater abundance. The Lord is beginning this deeper work of holiness in the lives of many of his messengers today.

As individuals, couples, and families, we have no choice but to make a serious commitment to separate ourselves from the values of the counter-kingdom. King David made such a determination: "I will walk in my house with blameless heart. I will set before my eyes no vile thing" (Ps 101:2-3). Can we decisively shut off the television at the Spirit's nudge, or stop a video that becomes offensive? Can we renounce excessive materialism and dabbling with sensuality? May God convict us of having become desensitized to the degradation of human dignity through cultural prejudice and violence. God forgive us for indulging in the idolatry of leisure. May God plant a desire in our hearts to honor and please him in our lifestyles.

Preparation for persecution and troubled times. At the close of each message to the churches, Jesus exhorts the recipients that the rewards of his kingdom will come to those who "overcome." Overcome what? The combined obstacles of world, flesh, and devil.

We are already seeing an increased pressure from the evil one that will manifest itself through earthly individuals and institutions. The worldly agenda promotes an enlightened "New Age," while planetary political winds blow us toward a "New World Order." Whether this particular phase continues or not, the concept of a global community is growing. These are days when discernment and wisdom must guide our witness in the midst of the world system. The enlightened child of God will feel increasingly out of step with the agenda. We are already seeing the intensity of such polarization. As one New Age writer put it bluntly, Christians and Jews will one day be "the problem"—stick-in-the-mud traditionalists with unyielding moral values.

Should we expect anything different? Paul bluntly warned Timothy, "... everyone who wants to live a godly life in Christ Jesus will be persecuted" (2 Tm 3:12). Christians will never fit into a system influenced by demonic powers and controlled by ungodly rulers. The coin of America's pluralistic society has two distinct sides. It provides for Christians the freedom to worship as we choose, but it also exacts the price of potential persecution because of the narrowness of the gospel message. An increased presence of the kingdom will inevitably provoke more violent persecution, which will then serve to more deeply purify and empower the remnant.

Living the good news exacts a price. Yet in the face of hardship, Paul thanks God "who always leads us in triumphal procession in Christ and through us spreads the fragrance of the knowledge of him" (2 Cor 2:14). The aroma is a fragrance to those who choose to believe, a stench of death to those who reject Christ as Lord. Believers are to some a blessing, to others an irritant. We're going to have to learn and live with the grace of the early Apostles that enabled them to love their enemies and endure hardship at their hands. As it was in the beginning days of the church, so will it be in the closing days.

A burden to pray for the Jews and Israel. I have observed a certain ignorance or blindness among many Christians that greatly troubles me. It is a lack of understanding God's sovereign dealing with his old covenant people, the Jews.

God made irrevocable promises to Israel and plans to fulfill them (Rom 11:25-32). The miracle of the re-establishment and re-settling of Israel and her survival in the midst of so much opposition should be proof enough.

I believe we will see in days ahead another increase of anti-

Semitism. Satan's age-old hatred of the Jews is, in fact, a stronghold of destruction. The body of Christ, the new covenant community, must rise to the place of intercession for the salvation of the Jews (see Rom 1:16) and the protection and peace of Jerusalem (Ps 122). Recently I found myself on a bus in Buenos Aires with a Jewish-Christian brother from Jerusalem. I was stricken by his words: "In World War II the church failed miserably to stand up for my people. I fear she will fail again when the world turns against Israel."

To pray for the Jews does not necessarily mean to condone everything the Israeli government does. But it does mean that we ask God to fulfull his purpose for his people. Biblically, a day will come when the "times of the Gentiles" is fulfilled, and God will deal fully and finally with the Jews. I believe we're approaching that transition. It is imperative that we pray in Jesus' authority for the salvation and protection of our old covenant brothers and sisters. Please, let's not fail again.

Let me add a final corrective to this discussion. There's a trap in strong end-time talk. I know it well, for over the years I've fallen into it quite regularly. Alarmism. Gloom and doomism. Frankly, I've had my fill of it. Let's be realistic about the resistance we know we face. But let's rejoice in the fact that we know the Lord of all creation and that we can live in his resurrection power. Can we have eyes to see that he who molded history *around* his chosen people is now ready to move the world *through* his chosen, both old and new covenant peoples? The day may soon come to look out ahead to the finish line, dig down deep, and find a surge of spiritual power to finish the race strong and hard.

THE SAINTS ARE STIRRING

Joe Aldrich is a most untypical Bible college president. As point man of Multnomah School of the Bible in Portland, Oregon, "Dr. Joe" is a visionary. In the late 1980s, he felt a growing burden for spiritual renewal among the pastors of the

Northwest. He and Terry Dirks, Joe's administrative pointman, created the Pastors Prayer Summit movement.

They met for the first time in February of 1989 at the Cannon Beach Conference Center with the pastors from the city of Salem. For four days, one "non-agenda" held sway: to seek fellowship with Jesus Christ in prayer and worship. Graciously, the Lord gave favor. A format developed for what has become a sustained and major movement of prayer among pastors.

Other cities and counties throughout the Northwest soon got wind of the movement. A formal ministry arm of Multnomah, Northwest Renewal Ministries, came into existence to train additional group facilitators. By 1990 interdenominational groups of pastors from cities all over the Northwest were experiencing the manifest blessing of God in these four-day gatherings.

I have been privileged to participate as a facilitator for some of these summits. In September, 1991, I helped lead a summit for the pastors of Clark County, Washington, along with Dick Palmer, a retired dentist dedicated to the prayer ministry. In addition to favoring us with four warm and sunny days (a most irregular event on the Oregon coast!), the Lord Jesus shone into the hearts of these pastors in a way which most of us had never experienced before.

———

*For years I had heard men in ministry give lip service
to such oneness, but here were men daring to practice and enjoy it.
We had gotten tired enough of ourselves, our programs,
playing at church. We were hungry for reality.*

———

Through unhurried sessions of worship, with the singing of choruses and hymns *a cappella*, spontaneous recitation of Scripture, and times of quiet waiting in silence, God graciously bestowed his blessing. His presence was so tangibly real. Doctrinal walls between conservative and charismatic, mainline and fundamentalist, denominational and independent, began to gently diminish in the manifest presence of Jesus.

This group of ministerial types, equipped with full array of pastoral personas, became as little children. We hurt when another hurt. We shared moments of hilarious laughter. We worshiped "in spirit and in truth." The heart of God seemed pleased to witness *his* people waiting on him, watching over *his* Word, yielded to *his* agenda.

This is how godly men are supposed to spend their time, giving "attention to prayer and the ministry of the word" (Acts 6:3). Jesus had come among us. On the third morning of the summit, we gathered for breakfast in a room overlooking the breathtaking vista of Cannon Beach. Something quite wonderful had happened. You could see it, hear it, sense it. These men truly loved one another! The earnest desire to preserve and sustain this precious oneness was clearly beginning to outweigh the pettiness of secondary doctrinal issues and denominational distinctives. For years I had heard men in ministry give lip service to such oneness, but here were men daring to practice and enjoy it. We had gotten tired enough of ourselves, our programs, playing at church. We were hungry for reality.

Is this a movement just for men? Certainly not. It is not meant to be exclusive or elitist, and in fact the idea is spreading to mixed groups. But in light of the strong needs of men to share transparently and bond deeply, these particular four-day gatherings have so far been limited to men. In this setting, these pastors are free to confess such struggles as pride, sexual lust, and inferiority. It seems that God himself sovereignly initiated this format so that men of God could find healing and build trust with other men.

The movement keeps gaining momentum. Requests for prayer summits arrive from cities across America. The sovereign seal of the Holy Spirit rests on these gatherings. Everyone involved is doing his and her best not to mess up the marvelous work the Lord is crafting! This is but one expression of his initiative to reclaim his people. He is doing a new thing in our midst. We are perceiving it. For anyone who has grown sick and tired of

cultural churchianity, God is making a way in the desert and providing streams in the wasteland (Is 43:19-20). Indeed, a sign of
hope.

Jesus is knocking at the door of the church, wanting to come
in to sup with us. Recently, forty-two pastors and leaders from my
county met at Cannon Beach for another four-day summit.
Within minutes of our beginning on a Monday afternoon, we sat
wrapped in God's presence. As Christians, we readily acknowledge that we are to walk by faith, not by sight or sensory stimuli.
But I still find myself reaffirmed and blessed when God chooses
to manifest himself in the midst of his people.

Not once did our leadership team struggle or strain to know
what to do. The Spirit of God sovereignly took charge, plunging
us deeper and deeper into a stripping process. Many pastors
released the rights to their callings and ministries. Openness
about struggles, confession of sin, and a disgust with self-effort
were as genuine as I have seen in these settings.

On the last night of this particular prayer summit, we entered
worship around the Lord's table. I grope for words to describe
the purity and power of what happened. The Holy Spirit perfectly orchestrated our praises, our prayers, our weeping, our
laughing. He led specific groupings of men to come to the table.
Some had come from the same town. Another group mixed
Baptists and charismatics in brotherly embrace. The youth pastors of our cities knelt together, recommitting themselves to
reach kids.

With each different group, the outer circle of men sang or
prayed the Lord's blessing upon those circled in communion.
Each time we imparted a Spirit-breathed blessing. No one person could have ever orchestrated this rising up of unity and
renewed faith. At one point, I sensed the Lord himself move on
our behalf to "take ground" in the heavenlies over our cities. I
recall thinking, *This is the way to do strategic spiritual warfare!* Paul
assured us that God would make known to the rulers and principalities the mystery of his will "through the church" (Eph 3:10).

In order for the watching world to believe in the viability of

Christ, believers must return to the vitality of life in Jesus. The stronghold called "separation and suspicion" holds the Lord's blessing at arm's length. Now is the time to open the door to Jesus, invite him in, and enjoy his presence.

Certainly this movement of the Spirit is not limited to pastors or clergy. I encourage you to participate in city-wide praise and prayer events. You can invite the Lord to break into your home fellowship or Bible study. My wife Terri recently started a Tuesday prayer group called "Watchwomen," featuring the simple practice of worship, waiting, and intercession guided by the Spirit of God. The hunger and readiness of the women has been encouraging.

A sovereign work of the Holy Spirit is underway to enable Christians to share a common fellowship in the Lord. Some are calling this "prerevival." If the glory of God is filling the temple, we are waiting anxiously in the foyer. I believe that soon the weight of intercessory prayer will compel God to manifest his presence in our midst, reviving and making ready his people for ministries of hope, harvest, and healing.

A REMNANT ON THE RISE

Consider this question. If Jesus were preparing for his return at a specific point in history, what would he begin to do in the hearts of his people prior to that return? If we are a bride awaiting the coming of the groom, can we not assume that he would desire, more likely demand, a holy bride? Would there not be deep, anticipatory stirrings within an excited bride who senses his nearness? Would there not be a growing desire in Jesus' own heart to claim and find joy in his bride?

This is not a book on prophecy. I'm not laying out a scenario of dates and events. I'm simply describing some of what I see happening among God's people—a repentant return to Jesus as our heart's desire and only source of hope. I see the Lord graciously at work reviving those of us who are weary of our own well doing and equipping us to better reach the lost. My own response to his redemptive heartbeat motivated this book.

I believe we are living in times of a parallel development: the outpouring of the Spirit of God in reviving, redeeming power, right alongside the building of a satanic world system inspired by spirits of the antichrist. God is lovingly alerting those with ears to hear, and giving us time to prepare for the spiritual warfare that lies ahead.

I believe we are living in times of a parallel development:
the outpouring of the Spirit of God in reviving, redeeming power,
right alongside the building of a satanic world system
inspired by spirits of the antichrist.

No one can be sure of the exact time frame in Daniel's mind when he wrote about "the time of the end," but the essence of his words is relevant to our times: "Many will be purified, made spotless and refined, but the wicked will continue to be wicked. None of the wicked will understand, but those who are wise will understand" (Dn 12:10).

Do we understand where we are? Sadly, many Christians seem to be in a stupor. We must heed the Apostle's warning *now:* "Let us not be like others, who are asleep, but let us be alert and self-controlled" (1 Thes 5:6)—vigilant, sober, and discerning the nature of our times. Jesus stands knocking at the door. Will we let him be Lord of his church?

The spiritual awakening currently underway in the Northwest is getting the attention of the secular press. One reporter wrote these reflections: "Growing evangelical fervor, coupled with a general feeling of alienation from institutions, makes America ripe for a religious revival, as people are turning to religion as they search for answers in a troubled time. One way to understand what could happen in a revival is to imagine that this country's religious community is a dried-out forest. All that's needed for a fire is a spark."[2]

While distinctive elements characterize this prayer movement in the Northwest, it is not isolated. God is raising up many models of spiritual renewal. Who can presume to keep up with him? Church, para-church, and missions organizations can hardly move fast enough to fill the requests for the gospel in what used to be the Soviet Union. With concerted emphasis on intercession and spiritual warfare, Argentina continues to experience phenomenal church growth.

In Los Angeles, the "LOVE L.A." movement was begun several years ago by Jack Hayford, international charismatic leader, and Lloyd Ogilvie, mainline pastor of First Hollywood Presbyterian Church. These two men became prayer partners and launched a vision to unite pastors in worship, prayer, and repentance. Evelyn Christenson, an author and leader in the women's prayer movement, reports unprecedented hunger in prayer meetings across America. Fern Nichols, founder of Moms in Touch, is seeing a virtual explosion of groups of mothers who gather to pray for their kids in the public schools.

David Bryant, originator of the current "Concerts of Prayer" movement, continues to lead mass city gatherings of Christians of all denominational labels in united prayer for awakening in the church. In May 1992, Bryant described the momentum of the prayer movement in America:

> Is it possible that God could kindle the fires of spiritual revival in our nation at this critical point in our history? In my travels around the country in recent months, I've witnessed an unprecedented grass-roots prayer movement that I'm convinced will prove to be the precursor of a sweeping moral and spiritual rebirth in America. Something extraordinary is taking place. It may be the most hopeful sign of our times.[3]

Tracing to a movement spawned in England by Graham Kendrick, cities around the world are participating in praise marches, giving verbal and visible witness to the lordship of Jesus. Plans are currently underway for the largest, most visible prayer gathering in the history of the church on June 24, 1994, in connection with the A.D. 2000 Movement and Beyond. Organizers are calling it "A Day to Change the World." This mass prayer gathering will be coordinated in major cities throughout the world and will send up a volume of intercession.

Dr. David McKenna, president of Asbury Theological Seminary, is convinced that a major awakening is coming, particularly among college students: "Is another Great Awakening on the way as we come to the close of the twentieth century? The answer is yes. We have the pattern of American history, the perspective of global revival, and the promise of God's word."[4]

In a word, the saints are stirring, the remnant is on the rise, the army is marching. Where all this is going, God alone knows. Historically, church revival has most often occurred in particular cities or geographical areas. What we are now witnessing is an outpouring of widespread proportions. The signs are unmistakable. God is renewing us in the power of his manifest presence. Why? To equip us for involvement in worldwide harvest.

THE KINGDOM CALLING

Our highest calling is to bring glory to God by loving him supremely and walking uprightly. In the wake of the televangelist scandals, the secularization of the church, and opposition from anti-Christian forces, let's seize this hour as an opportunity to reemphasize a timely witness to timeless truths. Until the final trumpet, our Redeemer is looking to purchase, with his own blood, people from every tribe and tongue and nation (Rv 5:9). Jesus is building his church and the gates of hell will not prevail against the plan of the ages.

Whether you are a homemaker or a career person, a businessman or a professional, a student or a politician, you mingle every day with a wide mix of people. The Lord is waiting to plant in the hearts of others the same seed of hope you carry within you. Many of us need some fresh encouragement, along with some new skills, to sow that seed purposefully and productively.

I believe opportunities for witness and harvest will literally explode upon us in the years ahead. If we stay close to our Lord's heart and listen for his voice, he will be pleased to use us in guiding his sheep to the fold. But to be so used, we must learn the regular practice of listening prayer. Prayer that originates in his will. Prayer that cares for "sheep number one hundred." Prayer that takes bold authority to beat back the wolves. Prayer that results in new names recorded in the Lamb's book of life.

10

A Call to Arms

AMONG TODAY'S MOST POPULAR PRAISE CHORUSES, one of my favorites clearly sounds the call to war: "Raise up an army, O God, alert your people throughout the earth." God's army is on the move. Our glorious Captain is raising leadership to rally the troops and lead them in the kind of prayer that will pierce the smoke screens of satanic strongholds.

If God is gracing his people with a movement of prayer and praise, what is to be our expectation? What is the object of our rising kingdom enthusiasm? What in the world do we expect our Lord to do? If God is raising an army, what's our assignment? Let me share a quotation from S.D. Gordon's *Quiet Talks on Prayer*. I would personally retitle this little book something like, *Raging Bonfires of Blinding Light on Spiritual Warfare Intercession*. Carefully ponder his words:

> Now prayer is a spirit force. It has to do wholly with spirit beings and forces. It is an insistent claiming, by a man, an embodied spirit being, down on the contested earth, that the power of Jesus' victory over the great evil-spirit chieftain shall extend to particular lives now under his control.

Prayer is man giving God a footing on the contested territory of this earth. The man in full touch of purpose with God praying, insistently praying—that man is God's footing on the enemy's soil. The man wholly given over to God gives Him a new sub-headquarters on the battlefield from which to work out. And the Holy Spirit within that man, on the new spot, will insist on the enemy's retreat in Jesus the Victor's name. That is prayer. Shall we not, every one of us, increase God's footing down upon His prodigal earth![1]

Our prayers can literally establish a command post in the midst of the satanic mess in which we live.

Our prayers can literally establish a command post in the midst of the satanic mess in which we live. Our challenge is to gain by faith footholds of righteousness, places infused with our Lord's presence. Our position in Christ grants us authority to insist on the retraction of Satan's rights in the fight for the salvation of men and women.

A good friend of mine serves as a counselor for victims of domestic violence and rape. I recently instructed her to saturate her efforts with prayers to combat the enemy's power. You can do the same wherever the Lord plants you. We have great biblical latitude in claiming persons for salvation. We can also legitimately target and tackle bigger and broader strongholds, even to liberate cities from enemy influence. I want this closing chapter to sound the trumpet for you to personally enter into the fray. First let's review some of the fundamental truths on the breaking of strongholds.

ENGAGING THE ENEMY

If we are to successfully wage this battle, we must first accurately identify the enemy and employ the weapons that overcome him. In the first chapter I defined a stronghold as "an entrenched pattern of thought, an ideology, value, or behavior that is contrary to the Word and will of God." This can range from a self-styled hedonism to such well organized philosophies as Scientology and secular humanism. The height of human pride expresses itself in an arrogant "Who needs God?" attitude of economic and scientific achievement.

Today's relativistic value system zealously guards each person's right to define and live his or her own reality. Those of us who live in Western culture are often more concerned with our rights and our material security than the rightness of an objective standard of truth. We also face strongholds, both human and demonic, of sensuality and violence. In order to pierce through these embattlements, we need to remember that strongholds operate on three levels:

- *The human mind:* doubt, deceit, unbelief, impurity (2 Cor 10:3-5)
- *Our culture:* self, power, violence, power, materialism (1 Jn 2:15-17)
- *Satan:* greed, deception, immorality, violence (Eph 6:10-12)

How can we distinguish between a stronghold that is of human origin or one that is satanic? Where do we draw a correct line between fleshly carnality and demonic corruption? Strongholds originated with the fall of Lucifer, but have taken root in human nature and culture. Frankly, we can only know where human impulse ends and satanic influence begins by sharpening our supernatural discernment. While the lines of demarcation can be hazy, repenting of ungodly values and behaviors in the church need not be so difficult. We must begin where we are by cleaning up our backyard, reforming our culture through revival, and giving satanic forces less to manipulate.

The premise of this book is that, as the redeemed of the Lord, we are called to radiate the reality of Jesus' love to others. The problem is that our own lenses are smudged. We cannot reflect a clear image of the Savior and his message. To be effective in setting captives free, it is imperative that we honestly look at our own strongholds, whether they be negative distortions of our identity in Christ or sin. Do what you need to do to close the doors on the devil's lies and live in the freedom Jesus alone can give.

We've also looked closely at strongholds that plague the corporate church. We've examined entrenchments of sin and wrong attitudes that rob the bride of her beauty and affect the church's appeal to a watching world. Pray for your church. If you see or suspect something amiss, pursue a pastor, elder, or deacon and pass on what you see. God is giving us light and authority to free our fellowships from satanic entanglements. We have allowed what seem to be innocent footholds to open the door to the enemy.

As you feel more of the Lord's burden for the lost, ask him to open your spiritual eyes to see the blindness and bondage that keep people from seeing Jesus. Make a decision to be available to the Lord to risk involvement in relating to and praying for people with new insight and authority. And choose to believe that God can and will teach you to hear his voice and give power to your prayers to restrain darkness and release light in others' lives.

I have also shared a vision for strategic spiritual warfare. This is not for everyone. Only those chosen and led of God to be involved in strategic warfare will know who the enemy is and when and how to assault strongholds. Only those who stay in the prayer closet long enough to receive instruction will have sufficient courage to lead the charge.

The bottom line is this: we can only go with what God gives us. And each one who moves into the arena of strategic warfare is responsible for his or her own leading and what results from it. It is difficult and dangerous to try to systematize something so intrinsically spiritual. God alone can be our mentor for strategic battle. We can only cultivate the ability to know what he is doing by deepening our personal intimacy with him. "Big praying" must begin with discipline and consistency in "little praying." Make prayer your central aim. No methodologies or strategies can ever substitute for true spirituality.

To whom do you look to know the mind of God? Whom do you listen to? Whom can you confidently and courageously follow in the pathways of intercessory prayer? These are big questions. That determination can only be yours. As we continue to "break trail" in this dimension in the years ahead, we would be wise to keep our eyes fixed on the pioneers of intercessory warfare. A call to arms requires that we look to and learn from our biblical models.

PIONEERS OF STRATEGIC INTERCESSION

Let's consider some biblical characters who were called to strategic, head-to-head encounters with evil powers and principalities. In Old Testament times, idolatry proved to be the major source of temptation for Israel. A multitude of false deities sought the attention and adulation of humankind. The second commandment states that "you shall have no other gods before me" (Dt 5:7), the implication being that other gods exist who do compete with the Almighty. In the face of competing deities, the people of Israel were challenged to keep their commitment to Yahweh. If they remained true to him, Yahweh the "Warrior" (Ex 15:3) would take care of Israel's enemies.

God himself chooses his vessels and then empowers them to confront his enemies. The following examples probably seem overwhelming. Looking at these heavyweights, God's mightiest warriors, can seem to leave you and me in the dust. But the Lord has now delegated his mighty authority to the church. Exposing and weakening Satan's henchmen is now *our* mandate.

Moses in the courts of Pharaoh. Yahweh instructed Moses to go to Pharaoh with the challenge to release Israel. We all know the story. Moses had already anticipated that Israel would not listen to him. Now he is given the charge to stand against the seat of authority in Egypt: "Moses said to the LORD, 'Since I speak with faltering lips, why would Pharaoh listen to me?' Then the LORD said to Moses, *'See, I have made you like God to Pharaoh,* and your brother Aaron will be your prophet'" (Ex 6:30-7:1, my emphasis).

We dare not, in our human strength,
go looking for strategic power encounters.
Any man or woman must hear the voice of the Lord and be sent.

This man of God felt emotionally and spiritually hesitant. Moses knew he was out of his league, but God gave him a divine power beyond himself. The assignment was to strike at a nation's power source. When Pharaoh took up the challenge and demanded a miracle, Aaron's staff turned into a snake. The magicians of Egypt then produced their own snakes! Yahweh countered by having Moses' snake devour the lesser serpents. The remaining plagues and Israel's miraculous deliverance through the Red Sea brought this power encounter to a dramatic conclusion.

Moses didn't go looking for an encounter with the powers of Egypt; he didn't want it and tried to argue his way out of it. Yet in the face of personal fear and inferiority, he submitted to God. In confronting Pharaoh, Moses and Aaron "did just as the LORD commanded them" (Ex 7:6). First, Moses heard the voice of God. Second, he was made to be "like God" to Pharaoh, that is, given an authority guaranteed to succeed. Third, Moses chose to obey and submit to the divine will. This example of Moses underscores a profound point: we dare not, in our human strength, go looking for strategic power encounters. Any man or woman must hear the voice of the Lord and be sent.

Elijah and the prophets of Baal. Elijah pulled off one of the most profound power encounters in biblical history (see 1 Kgs 18:16-46). The prophet brought the real issue into view: Who really is the Most High? At stake was the submission of Israel to Yahweh.

Elijah threw down a challenge to the prophets of Baal to demonstrate the power of their deities. The prophet, with taunts and mockery, then exposed the weakness of their god. He pressed them into a corner, with a holy boldness. Personally, I think the taunting part was more Elijah than the Spirit. We see here an example of the mixing of the divine mandate with the flaws of a man. Elijah's pride opened a crack for Jezebel's death curse to take hold in the form of subsequent self-pity. Even so, God was gracious to his servant and provided a way out.

Elijah then prepared a sacrifice to honor his God. But the key to the success of this encounter came with the prophet's boldness in prayer: "O LORD, God of Abraham, Isaac and Israel, let it be known today that you are God in Israel and that *I am your servant and have done all these things at your command.* Answer me, O LORD, answer me, so these people will know that you, O LORD, are God, and that you are turning their hearts back again" (1 Kgs 18:36-37, my emphasis).

Elijah's holy boldness was rooted in the clarity and confidence of God's command. He was prepared for, and indeed prompted, to issue this challenge. The Lord wanted to get his people's attention and break the power of Baal. He took the initiative to display the weakness of false gods and draw Israel back to obedience. Elijah was uniquely prepared and empowered. He had received an unmistakable word from God.

Having seen God validate his authority, Elijah still had to pay a personal price. Under a death threat by Ahab and Jezebel, "Elijah was afraid and ran" (1 Kgs 19:3). Humanly, this man suffered emotional exhaustion, the release of tension that follows a battle of this sort. It would be a mistake to analyze Elijah's demoralized decline only in emotional and psychological terms. We can assume that the spiritual forces associated with Baal worship were enraged and sought revenge.

Even so, I believe Elijah may have battled with some very human emotions. "Lord, I've done enough here, going out on a lonely limb for the honor of your name. I need a break." In the unguarded moment of human letdown, the powers of evil struck back at his weakness. For such a profound victory, the man of God paid a price.

Daniel and the satanic princes. Like Moses and Elijah, Daniel was uniquely chosen to participate in a strategic moment. Over the course of time, Daniel was given revelation on the history of his people, of the nations, and the coming of the Messiah. In the third year of Cyrus, King of Persia, another revelation came to Daniel during a prolonged fast.

A divine being—possibly the pre-incarnate Christ, but more probably Gabriel—came to Daniel in response to his plea for insight into a vision. Let's assume that it was Gabriel, the messenger angel. He revealed to Daniel the intensity of the spiritual battle: "But the prince of the Persian kingdom resisted me twenty-one days. Then Michael, one of the chief princes, came to help me, because I was detained there with the king of Persia" (Dn 10:13).

In the original Hebrew, the "prince of Persia" is unmistakably a territorial satanic angel on assignment to hinder transmission of the revelation. The outcome of the battle depends on the faithful service of the angels and the faithful response of a man of God in prayer. Verse 20 reveals the assignment of Gabriel and Michael to fight against these princes.

Daniel had nothing directly to do with the battle at that level. His role was to pray and submit to the will of God. The invisible battle raged on above and about him, being waged by the highest of the angels. Yet Daniel still experienced a significant struggle as he focused on the *person* of God and his *plan* for Israel, rather than on confronting the *powers of darkness*. Although aware that spiritual forces were involved, he remained devoted to prevailing prayer. Shouldn't this model inform and instruct our own practice of strategic warfare?

Scanning these Old Testament examples leads me to several conclusions concerning strategic warfare. These appointed and anointed vessels were sent into strategic battle by God's sovereign choice. They wrestled with the issue of submission. They were connected to the divine will through prayer. And each servant was committed to the glory of God.

What can we learn here? God must initiate our forays into strategic warfare. Who in their right mind would personally seek such a heavy burden, with such a steep price to pay? Let those called to spiritual warfare check their motives and get their signals clear. Let anyone who presumes to tackle the higher powers take note: he or she must be clearly led by God to do so.

Another instructive example is Jehoshaphat, a man who resisted evil and helped to reform Israel during a time of spiritual degradation. Because Jehoshaphat obeyed the Lord's command to remove the unholy high places and Asherah poles (2 Chr 17:1-6), fear of the Lord fell on the surrounding kingdoms. But even after a reign of twenty-five years, the high places were still not fully removed. Scripture tells us why: "The people still had not set their hearts on the God of their fathers" (2 Chr 20:33).

Our sustained participation is required to maintain our momentum. Otherwise, a strategic power encounter is an ill-advised endeavor.

Let's apply this principle to our own efforts in spiritual warfare. We can take significant initiatives to restrain evil strongholds, but the holiness of God's people must produce righteousness in our surrounding culture. This allows us to maintain the ground gained. More than any other man, Moses watched this principle play itself out with painful results. Disobedience on the part of the Israelites allowed the reinvasion of enemy influence.

Why should our experience be any different today? Any compromises we make with an immoral culture allow the powers of darkness to pollute the purity of God's kingdom within us. Our sustained participation is required to maintain our momentum. Otherwise, a strategic power encounter is an ill-advised endeavor.

Paul uses the "sword of the Lord." Let's conclude our survey of scriptural strategists with a New Testament example. After having violently opposed the man and message of Jesus, Saul of Tarsus was sovereignly stricken, led to salvation, and sent with a commission: "'Open their eyes and turn them from darkness to light, and from the power of Satan to God, so that they may receive forgiveness of sins and a place among those who are sanctified by faith in me'" (Acts 26:18).

Here again we see an unlikely vessel chosen and commissioned to oppose evil, with the primary object being the salvation of souls. This commission offers no hint of a holy crusade designed to cleanse the heavens of the polluting powers of hell. Paul is called to be involved in the miraculous mystery of building the church.

In his letter to the Ephesians, Paul portrays the wondrous miracle of God joining Jew and Gentile into one body and proclaims that God's wisdom and faithfulness are to "be made known to the rulers and authorities in the heavenly realms" (Eph 3:10). This tangible demonstration of divine community exposes the emptiness of evil. Dr. Clinton Arnold, a New Testament scholar, has captured well the essence of this key passage in Ephesians:

> This passage is not a warrant for raising a prophetic voice against the corrupted structures of our existence. In the context of Ephesians and of Pauline theology as a whole, the passage is merely asserting that the very existence of the church testifies to God's wisdom.... Both the existence of the church and the continued evangelistic growth of the church demonstrate to the powers that they are in fact powerless to impede the redemptive work of God.[2]

Further in the epistle, Paul addresses our ongoing struggle to stand against the relentless assault of evil (Eph 6:10-18). He exhorts us to employ spiritual armor for defense and divine weapons for offensive battle. How do we wage this war? Through the anointed presentation of truth (the *rema*, the sword of the

Spirit, the verbalized word) and the release of power in prayer.

Paul modeled this strategy when he confronted Elymas the magician on Cyprus. "You are a child of the devil and an enemy of everything that is right!" (Acts 13:10). As a sorcerer, this magician no doubt consorted with evil spirits. But Paul, led by the Spirit, spoke judgment upon the evil deeds of Elymas himself. We can only surmise that Paul's action certainly must have weakened the demonic power structure over the island of Cyprus.

After warning the church in Rome to watch out for those who cause division and strife, Paul injects a bold affirmation: "The God of peace will soon crush Satan under your feet" (Rom 16:20). Satan will be crushed under the feet of the body of Christ. But again it is *God* who will do the crushing.

THE MIXING OF WHEAT AND WEEDS

What form does this "crushing" of evil take? What is the kingdom going to look like in the closing years of this present age? What exactly are we praying toward? I began my introduction to this book with Jesus' words, "I will build my church and the gates of Hades will not overcome it" (Mt 16:18). That is precisely what is happening. The church is an ongoing, unfolding miracle!

But let's sharpen this picture with Jesus' parable of the weeds recorded in Matthew 13. Jesus told the story that the kingdom is like a farmer who has sown good wheat seed in his field. An enemy (the devil) tosses weed seed into the field, creating a messed up mix of wheat and weeds.

The farmer's servants want to immediately pull out all the weeds. The master stops them: "Let both grow together until the harvest" (Mt 13:30). Interpreting the parable for his disciples, Jesus sheds light on the state of the kingdom at the close of the age. As the weeds are pulled up and burned in the fire, so it will be at the end of the age. The Son of Man will send out his angels and they will weed out of his kingdom everything that causes sin and all who do evil.

The world harvest contains a mixed bundle, some for the

burn, some for the barn. Our Lord intends for his kingdom to grow up in the midst of the counterfeit kingdom of his adversary. We cannot be attached to the goal of reforming evildoers and institutions or even removing them. Yes, we should remain politically pro-active. We should stay committed to influencing our culture. *But our primary aim should be to water the seed that grows the wheat.*

The classic pre-millennialist believes that in the face of a worsening world condition and the rise of the system of the antichrist, Christians are to work hard at evangelism and expect an imminent rapture of the church that pulls us out of the picture. The kingdom cannot fully come until the King himself brings it. This position can lead to a limited perspective of the present power of the kingdom of God; it can create passivity, if not paralysis. The post-millennialist believes that the power of the gospel can and will reform society in the course of time. This perspective can lead to a false euphoria or overactivity.

What, then, does the kingdom look like? At any point in time, at any place, wherever his people are seeking to fully obey his commands and live worthy of his calling, *that is the kingdom.* At any point of history, its strength and presence may rise and fall, accelerate or deteriorate, depending on the spiritual condition of God's people and his sovereign initiatives.

I believe we can honestly pray and look for manifestations of the kingdom that powerfully transform particular cities and nations. Traditionally, we call this "revival." As the darkness gathers, God will establish "outposts of righteousness," special places of the light, the glory of his presence right in the midst of humanity's hopeless mess. We face major battles for cities, regions, and nations.

Does the breaking of evil strongholds precede revival, or does the breaking of human hearts precede the tearing down of strongholds? Jesus' own assessment offers a clue: "This is the verdict: Light has come into the world, but men loved darkness instead of light" (Jn 3:19). What good does it do to push back the enemy if the territory is not occupied by new forces? Penetration of strongholds that loosen the grip of false gods and proclamation of truth that leads souls to salvation must go hand in hand.

Recently I received a journal entitled *Crosswinds* put together by scholars and intercessors. I resonated especially with the thoughts of Dennis Peacocke, a Northern California pastor. He puts into economic language the moral bankruptcy of the modern world. He explains how this will lead to increased harvest for the kingdom:

> The secular state promised its citizens that it would support them and gave them a virtual blank check for their so-called "rights." God is cashing that check, knowing that it will bounce. When it falls back to earth, God will use the pressures of man's bankruptcy to arouse the church into redemptive action and harvest. A revival is coming amidst the debris of man's apostasy and desperation.[3]

I find this to be a word of hope. In the face of human culture adrift from the mooring of godly values, the church will have unparalleled opportunities to live the kingdom. Our primary call will be to demonstrate that only the love of the Lord and obedience to his commands can meet people's needs. Sure, the shadows of satanic darkness are lengthening. Yes, we can expect persecution for our "peculiar" kingdom ways. And yet we can also expect that in response to our prayers and obedience, the Ancient of Days will establish places of his presence in the very midst of his enemies.

WHO ME? YES *YOU!*

God has a habit of picking flawed and fickle people to do his bidding and be about his business. Moses and Jeremiah couldn't talk too well, Gideon had an anxiety problem, Samson had Delilah, David had Bathsheba. Solomon got carried away with his own power, Peter was impulsive, Paul had a "thorn," and

John Mark failed in his first two ministry assignments.

Guess what? God chooses men and women who are flawed, who have foibles, and who sooner or later fumble the ball. That means *you* qualify for the King's service! God uses peculiar people. And he is recruiting now for an end-of-the-age operation to rescue people out of the clutches of Satan's counter-kingdom. He is looking for imperfect people with a passion for his presence and a commitment to obey his word.

God chooses men and women who are flawed,
who have foibles, and who sooner or later fumble the ball.
That means you *qualify for the King's service!*

Perhaps you could start an outreach Bible study in your college dorm or neighborhood. Or join a prayer group serious about interceding for your city. Or volunteer your time at a crisis pregnancy counseling center to share wisdom and compassion with women facing a serious dilemma. Some of you might have a bent for politics and governmental decision-making. Go for it. The opportunities to practice redemptive prayer are endless.

Others may have a heart for harvest but are also highly gifted in accounting, engineering, medical care, or computer technology. You could possibly invest your dollars in a mission to the unreached or look for an overseas "tentmaking" opportunity. As wheat, we need to stay in the field, looking for new wheat seeds about to germinate. A door of unparalleled opportunity is now open. Seek the Lord for how he wants to touch others through you.

Many of us recall the words spoken at the beginning of each episode of the television series *Mission Impossible:* "Your assignment... should you choose to accept it...." Reaching a stony-hearted, disinterested relative or neighbor or business associate can certainly look like mission impossible. Getting the gospel to the unreached multitudes around the world can look absolutely overwhelming. But in the words of a spiritual warrior from another time, "... the battle is the LORD's" (1 Sm 17:47). When God gives an assignment, he also gives authority and anointing to carry it out.

You may be a sincere believer just discovering your new passion for prayer, just now asking the question, "Lord, where do I fit in this?" Many of you are probably dealing with the same issues I have wrestled with—the fear of rejection, feeling like I'm imposing my faith on others, or feeling inadequate in sharing the message. Some of you with a shy temperament may find it incredibly difficult to talk to strangers.

Whoever you are, wherever you are, the Lord wants to simply open your eyes to see the harvest field. He also wants you to feel some righteous anger toward the evil one who is so busily sowing weed seed. I'm convinced God can teach every one of us how to pray with insight and authority, how to watch for divine appointments, and how to open doors. Let me suggest three simple check points for involvement in the harvest.

Check your spiritual pulse. In a simple paraphrase, Jesus challenged his hearers that our greatest responsibility and fulfillment is to love God with all our being. That's where we begin.

The church at Ephesus grieved the Lord because they had wandered from the fervency of their first love. Are you too busy, too distracted, too involved in church work, to give God the best of who you are, to bless him with your worship? What he most wants for you and me is a more intimate relationship. Our God is incurably relational! If you're stuck in any sin that hinders your fellowship with him, get it right. Bring it to the cross. He is so quick to forgive.

Do you love yourself? Have you settled into the unshakable assurance of God's fatherly favor toward you? Or do you wrestle with the agonies of self-accusation, self-doubt, inferiority, and comparison with others? Without reservation, I can say that the Lord wants to heal you of any lingering pain of rejection or performance pressure. If this area provides a chink in your armor, pursue a path that leads toward healing.

Do you love your neighbor? This is a big one. Some of you need to pray about this, and ask God to give you his heart for people who are different, or whom you just don't like. Are you really convinced that without Christ people run the risk of inheriting the horrors of an eternal hell? The Lord wants to give you an assignment to love someone into his kingdom, should you choose to accept it.

Resolve personal issues. The Lord uses imperfect people. That is true in the Scriptures and it remains true today. But his will is that we be walking in obedience and pressing toward a life of increasing victory. If you're dragging a ball and chain, or sitting on the sidelines as a member of the disabled list, face your sin and deal with it. Too many good players are left hanging in the shadows of service, because they are stuck in guilt over their anger, bitterness, mental impurities, and overindulgence. The power of God through prayer and faith can break the chains and deal with those disabilities. He wants each one of us to be fulfilled and fruitful.

Get a vision. Our crucial need for vision sounds so well-worn, even trite. But it remains central. Sometimes we need to look at the big picture to understand the small picture. Our earthly life is so very temporary. Anyone can be history in a second in a head-on collision. Your heart could stop tomorrow. Catch a glimpse of the reality of eternity and hold onto it. Let the seeking first of his kingdom and his righteousness grip you and compel you into finding your niche.

I know of no more exciting time to be about the King's business than today. Keep watching. The Lord is restoring his people to purity and power. And he is going to put sovereign pressure on the masses of men and women through economic and natural calamity, disillusionment with political systems, and the terrors of pestilence and war. For such a time as this you have been born. Don't catch yourself sleeping through the greatest harvest in redemptive history.

A FORETASTE OF HEAVEN

Haven't we all tried to imagine what heaven will be like? Such a vision brings hope to our heavy hearts and gives purpose to our pains and perplexities. God promises that heaven will be far better and brighter than we can imagine or even believe (1 Cor 2:9). This life, with all its joys and fulfillments, just doesn't make it. The deepest longings of the heart go unsatisfied, justice goes undone, our questions unanswered, and peace among peoples remains elusive.

Only the reality of a heaven can make sense of the hell many endure on earth. Only the love of the Lord can meet our deepest needs, heal our pains, answer our perplexities, balance the scales, and resolve our conflicts. Most of you reading this believe in heaven and have assurance of a place there. You've received forgiveness and the free gift of life in Jesus Christ.

But while pondering the glories of heaven brings hope to our hearts, we should also pause to consider the pain of those who won't be there. Anyone who takes the Bible seriously has to accept the reality of hell. Not a pleasant topic. But the Bible says that those who reject the Son outright and spurn God's gift of grace are destined for separation from the light of his presence.

———

Our Captain is sounding a call to arms, raising an army, and positioning us for an outpouring of his presence and power to reveal Jesus to other pilgrims still lost in the woods.

———

In the ugliness of his jealousy, Satan has served as God's archenemy down through the ages. "He was a murderer from the beginning, not holding to the truth, for there is no truth in him … he is a liar, and the father of lies" (Jn 8:44). Satan rages in an unholy, vengeful passion to undermine the dignity of life and destroy humanity.

Back in the sixties, in my wandering days, Satan nearly succeeded in destroying me. When I came to my senses and God graciously received me into his loving arms, I vowed to expose the devil's lies and liberate others from his snares. The stakes are high. Are you ready to take a step further into the battle? Satan is pulling out the stops, greedily going after men, women, and kids. But our Captain is sounding a call to arms, raising an army, and positioning us for an outpouring of his presence and power to reveal Jesus to other pilgrims still lost in the woods.

As we look toward the end of this age—whenever that may come—God is giving us a taste of his holiness and his glory, so that in the dark times of testing ahead, we will not be tempted to be satisfied with anything less than himself. God wants to recapture his church. He will redeem his old covenant people, Israel. The Bridegroom wants to clean up his sin-stained bride and empower her as a witness to the world.

In some recent prayer gatherings, I have seen God visit his people in tremendous power. We are hearing reports from around the world that he is pouring out his presence in the midst of prayer and praise. In the spiritual warfare that lies ahead, we will need to remember the taste, the touch, and the texture of God's presence. The fleeting glimpses of his glory in the good times will enable us to keep our gaze fixed on him in the hard times.

In the eighteenth century, the Lord raised up Jonathan Edwards to begin a movement of prayer that preceded America's First Great Awakening. Edwards captured a vision of what he called "united, concerted prayer" by reading Zechariah 8:18-23. I believe God wants to give us that same kind of vision to enable the messianic kingdom to come, to be literally realized in Jerusalem and the land of God's favor. He calls his people to fasting as "joyful and glad occasions and happy festivals for Judah." Many peoples from many cities are called together to pray and to say, "let us go at once to entreat the LORD and seek the LORD Almighty."

The final verse in this prophetic text points toward God's fulfillment of his purposes for and through Israel: "This is what the LORD Almighty says: "In those days ten men from all languages and nations will take firm hold of one Jew by the hem of his robe and say, 'Let us go with you, because we have heard that God is with you.'"

The fulfillment of Zechariah's vision is in the future for Israel. And yet I believe this can be a type or model for united, faith-filled prayer that gives the church and the watching world a fore-taste of the goodness and glory of God. In the midst of a secular culture, facing satanic enemies on every side, we the people of God need to know beyond doubt that God is with us. And we need to understand that the outpouring of his blessed presence on our prayer gatherings will create a yearning in other people's hearts to find out what we are about.

Even in comparison with all of life's chills and thrills, bells and whistles, nothing is more exciting than walking through life with the King of the universe. This is the best bottom line there is. I've shared many illustrations and exciting stories. You've read inspiring quotations from men and women of great faith. Maybe you've been touched and stirred a bit, perhaps built up in your own faith.

Now I want to put the pressure on you. You can do this. You too can live the mystery of Jesus living his life through you. You can learn to hear his voice and read his signals. You can be an ambassador on assignment. It can be so supernaturally natural. Let the Lord Jesus have all of you. Let him give you the fullness of his Spirit. In all the splendors of the heavenly kingdom, no joy will be greater than looking across the glassy sea in the midst of a massive praise gathering, and seeing the face of a neighbor, a co-worker, or a student who is there because of your obedience. The harvest is ripe. Today is the day of salvation.

In view of the reality of Jesus' sure return, Paul prayed for the believers at Thessalonica. This is my prayer for you:

> (I) constantly pray for you, that our God may count you wor-thy of his calling, and that by his power he may fulfill every good purpose of yours and every act prompted by your faith. (I) pray this so that the name of our Lord Jesus may be glori-fied in you, and you in him, according to the grace of our God and the Lord Jesus Christ. **2 Thes 1:11, 12**

NOTES

ONE
Setting Prisoners Free: A Missing Dimension

1. Timothy Warner, *Spiritual Warfare* (Wheaton, Illinois: Crossway Books, 1990), 15.
2. Tom White, *The Believer's Guide to Spiritual Warfare* (Ann Arbor, Michigan: Servant Books, 1990).
3. George Otis, *The Last of the Giants* (Tarrytown, New York: Chosen Books, 1991), 85.
4. Otis, 89.
5. Douglas Groothuis, *Unmasking the New Age* (Downers Grove, Illinois: InterVarsity Press, 1986) and *Confronting the New Age Movement* (Downers Grove, Illinois: InterVarsity Press, 1988). Russell Chandler, *Understanding the New Age* (Irving, Texas: Word Publishing, 1988).

TWO
Breaking Strongholds in Our Own Backyard

1. Jessie Penn-Lewis, *Soul and Spirit* (Dorset, England: Overcomer Publications), 23.
2. James Robison, "The Structure of Strongholds," *Charisma*, August, 1991, 54.

THREE
Hearing from Heaven

1. Norman Grubb, *Rees Howells: Intercessor* (Ft. Washington, Pennsylvania: Christian Literature Crusade, 1970), 252.
2. Andrew Murray, *Waiting on God* (Chicago: Moody Press, 1987), 29.
3. A.W. Tozer, *The Pursuit of God* (Camphill, Pennsylvania: Christian Publications, 1982), 17.
4. Watchman Nee, *The Spiritual Man* (New York: Christian Fellowship Publishers, 1968). Thomas à Kempis, *The Imitation of Christ* (New York: Sheed & Ward, 1959). Jeanne Guyon, *Experiencing the Depths of Jesus Christ* (Auburn, Maine: SeedSowers Christian Books, 1975).
5. J. Oswald Smith, *The Passion for Souls* (Burlington, Ontario: Welch Publishing Co., 1984), 59.

FOUR
From Bootcamp to the Trenches

1. Donald Posterski, *Reinventing Evangelism* (Downers Grove, Illinois: InterVarsity Press, 1989), 77.
2. *National & International Religion Report*, Vol. 6, No. 22, October 19, 1992.
3. Dennis Peacocke, "Discipling Our Cities: A Practical Strategy for Service," *Crosswinds*, Vol. 1, No. 1, Winter, 1992.

FIVE
Helping People Turn from Darkness to Light

1. S.D. Gordon, *Quiet Talks on Prayer* (Westwood, New Jersey: Barbour and Co., Inc., 1984), 33.
2. Evelyn Christensen, *Battling the Prince of Darkness* (Wheaton, Illinois: Victor Books, 1990), 102.
3. Wesley Duewel, *Mighty Prevailing Prayer* (Grand Rapids, Michigan: Francis Asbury Press, 1990), 233.

SEVEN
Understanding Strategic Warfare

1. Otis, 88.
2. Francis Frangipane, *The House of the Lord* (Lake Mary, Florida: Creation House, 1991), 55.
3. Frangipane, 122.

EIGHT
Watching over Our Cities

1. Dick Eastman, *Love on Its Knees* (Tarrytown, New York: Chosen Books, 1989), 65.
2. David Mains and Steve Bell, *Two Are Better than One* (Portland, Oregon: Multnomah Press, 1991).
3. Paul's apostolic prayers are found in Ephesians 1:15-19 and 3:14-21; Colossians 1:1-9; Philippians 1:9-11; and 2 Thessalonians 1:11-12.

NINE
Ready for Outpouring

1. Helen Howarth Lemmel, "Turn Your Eyes Upon Jesus," *Inspiring Hymns* (Grand Rapids, Michigan: Sacred Music Publishers, 1951), No. 379.
2. Tom Hallman, Jr., *The Oregonian*, August 2, 1992.
3. David Bryant, "National & International Religion Report," Special Report, May 1992.
4. David McKenna, *The Coming Great Awakening* (Downers Grove, Illinois: Inter-Varsity Press, 1990), 10.

TEN
A Call to Arms

1. Gordon, 35.
2. Dr. Clinton Arnold, *The Powers of Darkness*, (Downers Grove, Illinois: Inter-Varsity Press, 1992), 197.
3. Peacocke, 31.

BIBLIOGRAPHY

LEARNING TO PRAY AND LISTEN TO GOD

Carson, D.A. *A Call to Spiritual Reformation.* (Grand Rapids, Michigan: Baker Book House, 1992).

Duewel, Wesley. *Mighty Prevailing Prayer.* (Grand Rapids, Michigan: Zondervan, 1990).

Guyon, Jeanne. *Experiencing the Depths of Jesus Christ.* (Gardiner, Maine: Christian Books, 1981).

Huggett, Joyce. *The Joy of Listening to God.* (Downers Grove, Illinois: InterVarsity, Illinois, 1986).

Willard, Dallas. *The Spirit of the Disciplines.* (San Francisco, California: Harper & Row, 1988).

SPIRITUAL WARFARE
General

Anderson, Neil T. *Victory over the Darkness.* (Ventura, California: Regal Books, 1990).

Arnold, Clinton. *Powers of Darkness.* (Downers Grove, Illinois: InterVarsity Press, 1992).

Kraft, Charles. *Christianity with Power.* (Ann Arbor, Michigan: Servant Publications, 1989).

Murphy, Ed. *The Handbook for Spiritual Warfare.* (Nashville, Tennessee: Thomas Nelson, 1992).

Sherman, Dean. *Spiritual Warfare for Every Christian.* (Seattle, Washington: Frontline Communications, 1990).

Sherrer, Quin and Garlock, Ruthanne. *A Woman's Guide to Spiritual Warfare.* (Ann Arbor, Michigan: Servant, 1991).

Warner, Timothy. *Spiritual Warfare.* (Wheaton, Illinois: Crossway Books, 1991).

Practical

Anderson, Neil T. *The Bondage Breaker.* (Eugene, Oregon: Harvest House, 1990).

Bubeck, Mark. *The Adversary.* (Chicago, Illinois: Moody Press, 1975).

Bubeck, Mark. *Overcoming the Adversary.* (Chicago, Illinois: Moody Press, 1984).

Carty, Jay. *Counterattack.* (Portland, Oregon: Multnomah Press, 1988).

Koch, Kurt. *Occult Bondage and Deliverance.* (Grand Rapids, Michigan: Kregel Publications, 1976).

White, Tom. *The Believer's Guide to Spiritual Warfare.* (Ann Arbor, Michigan: Servant Publications, 1990).

Strategic

Christenson, Evelyn. *Battling the Prince of Darkness.* (Ventura, California: Victor Books, 1990).

Dawson, John. *Taking Our Cities for God.* (Lake Mary, Florida: Creation House, 1990).

Eastman, Dick. *Love on Its Knees.* (Old Tappan, New Jersey: Fleming H. Revell Co., 1989).

Frangipane, Francis. *The House of the Lord.* (Lake Mary, Florida: Creation House, 1991).

Gordon, S.D. *Quiet Talks on Prayer.* (Westwood, New Jersey: Barbour & Co., 1984).

Johnstone, Patrick. *Operation World.* (Fort Washington, Pennsylvania: Christian Literature Crusade, 1970).

Otis, Jr., George. *The Last of the Giants.* (Tarrytown, New York: Chosen Books, 1991).

Wagner, Elizabeth. *Tearing Down Strongholds: Prayer for Buddhists.* (Kowloon, Hong Kong: Christian Literature Crusade, 1988).

Wagner, C. Peter. *Engaging the Enemy.* (Ventura, California: Regal Books, 1991).

Wagner, C. Peter. *Warfare Prayer.* (Ventura, California: Regal Books, 1992).

BREAKING EMOTIONAL STRONGHOLDS

Backus, William. *Telling Truth to Troubled People.* (Minneapolis, Minnesota: Bethany House, 1985).

Frank, Jan. *A Door of Hope.* (San Bernadino, California: Here's Life Publishers, 1987).

Payne, Leanne. *The Broken Image.* (Westchester, Illinois: Crossway Books, 1981).

Seamands, David. *Healing Grace.* (Wheaton, Illinois: Victor Books, 1988).

THE NEW AGE MOVEMENT

Chandler, Russell. *Understanding the New Age.* (Waco, Texas: Word, 1988).

Groothuis, Douglas. *Unmasking the New Age Movement.* (Downers Grove,

Illinois: InterVarsity Press, 1986).

Groothuis, Douglas. *Confronting the New Age Movement.* (Downers Grove, Illinois: InterVarsity Press, 1988).

RESOURCES

Spiritual Counterfeits Project Newsletter, P.O. Box 4308, Berkeley, CA.

Concerts of Prayer International, Pentagon Towers, P.O. Box 36008, Minneapolis, MN, 55435. Directed by David Bryant; materials on leading corporate, united prayer.

Freedom in Christ Ministries, 491 East Lambert Rd., LaHabre, CA, 90631. Directed by Neil Anderson and Timothy Warner; materials and ministry on truth encounter and spiritual warfare.

Every Home for Christ, P.O. Box 3590, Colorado Springs, CO, 80935-3593. Directed by Dick Eastman; provides materials on intercessory prayer, particularly for unreached peoples.

Christian Research Institute, Box 500, San Juan Capistrano, CA 92693. Research on cults and the occult; regular newsletter, quarterly journal.

The Sentinal Group, P.O. Box 6334, Lynnwood, WA, 98036. George Otis, Jr.; materials on strategic prayer for unreached nations.

Frontline Ministries, P.O. Box 786, Corvallis, OR 97339. Teaching and training on strategic spiritual warfare and intercession. Cassette tapes and other materials available.

Other Books of Interest from Servant Publications

The Believer's Guide to Spiritual Warfare
Tom White

The Believer's Guide to Spiritual Warfare offers biblically sound, accurate, and balanced teaching on the unseen war being waged around us. Complete with real-life illustrations, sample prayers, proven techniques, and answers to the most commonly asked questions about warfare, this book will help believers to fulfill a central call of the gospel—to resist evil with the power and authority of the cross. *$8.99*

A Woman's Guide to Spiritual Warfare
Quin Sherrer with Ruthanne Garlock

Women everywhere face battles that threaten to overwhelm them and those they love. What can women do in the face of such monumental difficulties? *A Woman's Guide to Spiritual Warfare* shows how they can work with God to change the course of their lives and the lives of family and friends. *$8.99*

Defeating Dark Angels
Charles H. Kraft

In *Defeating Dark Angels* Charles Kraft explains how demons operate, how to resist their influence, and how to cast them out in Jesus' name. Here is the practical and spiritual help Christians need, both to defeat dark angels in their own lives and to minister God's freedom and healing to others. *$8.99*